PUBLIC SPEAKING:

EXCITE, ENGAGE AND ENTERTAIN

33 WAYS TO KEEP YOUR AUDIENCE ON THE EDGE OF THEIR SEATS

Mark Davis

Table of Contents

Preface. 1

Solve the problem. 4

From beginning to end. 7

Entertainment. 9

Get involved. 13

Location, location. 19

The mirror. 28

Just one person. 31

Speaking activities. 33

The blessed silence. 36

Entertaining stories. 40

Breaking the ice. 47

Keywords and sound bites. 50

Questions? 55

Say it again. 61

Reflection. 66

Summary. 70

Writing activities. 73

More writing activities. 77

Mission statements, goals and plans. 81

Drawing. 83

Numbers. 86

Partner activities. 88

Competitions...91

Volunteers...96

Role play..100

Shaking hands...103

How to spend a million dollars.....................................106

Handouts. 110

Physical activities. 114

The power of a smile. 119

How to get a standing ovation. 125

The treasure hunt. 128

Visuals and props. 131

Multimedia. 138

Apps and software. 141

Photos. 145

Objections...148

The end. 151

What next?..153

Preface.

Bore the audience. They will remember you always, but not fondly.

You have a great opening.

You have a great close.

The long minutes between the opening and close ... better be good. Audiences aren't very forgiving.

They want to be excited and motivated. They want a reason to keep listening.

Audiences want entertainment. They can get our information in a book or website, but that is boring. They want to be personally entertained by us.

Good speakers engage the audience's attention through entertaining stories, activities and content. We should use interactive activities, games, exercises and more.

Make public speaking a memorable experience and your audience will love you.

- Nervous about silence?
- Uncomfortable with asking the audience questions?
- Afraid of letting your listeners talk to each other?
- Don't know how to start a game or exercise?

Relax.

Get ready to discover some simple ways to make our talk interesting and memorable. All of these will help you to remove the fear of losing the audience's attention.

And most are five minutes or less, so they are easy to learn and implement.

Thank you for reading this book. Here are two quick resources as a gift to you.

#1. Here is a free training audio to help you with your public speaking. Just go to this site to download it now: http://www.markdavis.com.au

#2. Get notified when the next new public speaking book is released by subscribing at this website: http://www.mastertheartofpublicspeaking.com

If you would like a public speaking workshop in your city or for your group, contact Coach Mark Davis directly at:

Mark@MasterTheArtOfPublicSpeaking.com

Solve the Problem.

Ten minutes into my talk, and there was trouble brewing. I came after the speaker who was so boring that the tech guy turned off his microphone to help him finish.

Looking around the room, it seemed hopeless.

I was the last speaker before the afternoon tea break. The low blood sugar levels made the audience tired and irritated. They wanted sweets and sugar, **now**.

Some people had already drifted off to sleep. An old man in the second row was snoring loudly.

Even the hecklers in the back corners had given up heckling me. Too much effort from the back of the room.

Screeching chairs announced that many audience members were leaving for the toilets or for an early place in line for the snacks.

The remaining audience made eye contact with their phones.

It was a disaster zone.

No point blaming the previous speaker. This was here and now. My survival clock was ticking faster and faster.

- Should I try and tell a joke?
- Maybe get everyone to stand up and yell?

- Do I just talk louder?
- Tell a funny story?

Create your disaster plan BEFORE the disaster arrives.

We all fear these worst-case scenarios. That is why public speaking makes us nervous.

But that fear can go away if we have a disaster plan that addresses the bad events and situations that will occur in our speaking career.

Wouldn't you feel better if you already knew exactly what to do to keep your audience engaged? And that is the purpose of this book.

To keep our audience interested from beginning to end.

We want to control our audience by delivering great value and interactivity. We don't want our audience and outside circumstances to determine the success of our speech.

In this book we will learn how to keep the audience engaged with techniques such as:

- Entertaining games.
- Personalized storytelling.
- Sound bites and key words.
- Volunteering opportunities.
- Exciting competitions.
- Group activities.
- Role play.

Yes, we need a plan to consistently entertain our audience. The audience will remember us, but we want them to remember us fondly!

Plus, we will no longer fear the front row snoring, the previous bad speaker, or the bored heckler. Instead, we will simply execute the appropriate technique from our tool chest of audience engagement.

Make the audience love us.

We want to deliver our message. So why not excite, entertain and engage the audience while we deliver?

Giving a TED talk, a wedding speech or a sales pitch? You will love this book.

Let us get started now to learn exactly how to create a great talk from beginning to end.

From Beginning to End.

We have a great opening. We have practiced our closing sentences. What about the time between the opening and the closing? This is when we want to be the most entertaining. We want the audience to find us interesting. And beyond being informative, we need to keep our audience awake.

This is the middle of the talk.

The best meetings and presentations are remembered fondly when they are entertaining and engaging.

When we are speaking, we need to work on having a conversation with our audience. We do not want to talk "at" them or make them feel like the talk is one-sided.

Remember,

1. The audience is setting aside time to listen to us, so we must provide value in every moment.

2. They value entertainment over serious lectures.

Let us look at the three key principles of this book.

Excitement.

The emotional state of our audience is under our control. If we do a good job, they will make decisions to like us and continue to listen to us.

Do it well, and the feeling in the crowd will be infectious. Everyone will have a good time.

People sit on the edge of their seat when they have an emotional connection and are getting value from the speaker.

Entertainment.

Giving everyone in our audience a good time is the key to entertaining them. This has to be part of our philosophy when we stand up onstage to present. Salespeople know that the best sales come when the prospects are happy and enjoying themselves.

Engagement.

We engage with our audience to make sure we gain rapport, and keep it.

This happens at the beginning when we open our presentation. But it is also necessary during the middle and all the way to the end of our talk.

If we can master these two areas, our talk will be remembered positively, and at the close of our talk, we will get the results we want.

This book will show many ways to accomplish this.

Entertainment.

All speakers can learn
the art of entertainment.

Salespeople need to have good presentations. They have to keep the prospect or client interested long enough to get to a close and a decision to buy.

Network marketers use their passion for their business and their products. The benefits of time and money freedom create numerous stories and transformations.

The best man giving a wedding speech relies on jokes and anecdotes about his friendship with the groom to make the audience laugh.

All of these presentations require an "entertainment" factor.

Entertainment is about the audience having a good time. We have to work to provide it, but a happy crowd is our responsibility. When we make this our goal, we learn to be more interesting.

Here is a reminder we need to plaster all over our preparation notes whenever we think that facts and figures are more important than being interesting and entertaining.

Entertainers are the highest-paid individuals on the planet.

Be a good entertainer, and we can increase our income.

Be a good entertainer, and we will be popular.

Be a good entertainer, and we will be in demand as a speaker.

A note about being funny.

Most people are not born funny. And it is not usually something that is spontaneous or natural either.

Being funny is something that takes work. Jokes require planning and timing. Performing standup comedy and working out what an audience finds funny is difficult.

Jerry Seinfeld says it takes him up to 300 minutes of preparation for a 6-minute set. That is a lot of work for such a short period of time. But the results? When it is funny, it is **really** funny. And we all quote and tell stories about the performance for days, weeks, even years to come.

Jim Carrey is funny. His rubber-faced impressions and over-the-top hilarity are mistaken as childish, but we love them because we laugh like a child. But he was in the comedy and movie wilderness for years before being "discovered" and getting the movie, *Ace Venture: Pet Detective*.

Robin Williams had an intense, rapid-fire humour that would hit again and again until no defenses could withstand him. In interviews he was funny. On the stage he was funny. On the big and small screen he was funny. Mrs. Doubtfire, Hook, Mork and Mindy.

Amy Poehler and Tina Fey are an amazing combination of comediennes that deliver laugh after laugh together. Again, the preparation time for the jokes - written by other people - and their timing and delivery show the work involved in giving a great performance. Even then the laughs are not guaranteed. But they spend the time, and so the chances of being funny and getting the laughs they want are in their favour.

Using humour in our talk helps the audience relax. Laughing releases oxytocin and serotonin into the blood, giving people a feeling of well-being. And they come to like the person that gave them that feeling.

When the audience is relaxed, they are more receptive to what we have to say.

Our message should always be easy to understand. When we use humour, the audience relaxes. This makes it easier for them to remember our message.

Here are a few ways to promote a relaxed atmosphere:

- Look at our life experiences with a light-hearted view.
- Find the humour in current situations and share it.
- Be the person that is positive and laughs at problems and challenges.
- Have the attitude that people are unique and interesting and entertaining.
- Create a memory for the audience.

There are plenty of books just about humour and being funny. Here it is just a part of what we can use to be more entertaining for our audience.

Entertainment is a skill
we need to work on.

We will be remembered, but not for our logical presentation and perfect fonts in our PowerPoint.

What the audience remembers is:

- A story they laugh at.
- A statistic they have never heard before.
- An intriguing statistic.
- An experience they have during the talk that is interactive.
- A movie or slide they see that triggers a memory.
- A new app for their phone they installed.
- Taking a new type of photo.
- Posing for a photo with the speaker.
- Observing a volunteer.
- Sharing something they never knew before.
- Being surprised.
- Being involved.
- Receiving valuable new knowledge.

Let us look at some entertainment strategies, starting with stories.

Get Involved.

Have you ever read a book and wished that it had an alternate ending?

Or have you read a book and been so involved that you felt you were the star?

You're at the edge of the cliff.

1. If you jump off into the river below, turn to page 87.
2. If you start climbing down the cliff, turn to page 74.

The "Choose your own adventure" series of books gave control of the action to the young reader. And they created a multi-million-dollar market for interactive books worldwide. For the first time, children could read a book 10 times and have a different adventure every time!

Of course the best part of the book was … the reader was the star. So instead of simply reading, they were living the book! Now the kids that were never reading were desperate to go to bed. Then they could continue the adventure or start a new one.

We need to understand and apply the principle of creating compelling content. Beyond this, we need to develop stories, presentation slides and activities to create a talk that involves the audience. By being entertaining, we can have the audience wanting to participate.

This will make the speaking or presenting experience something the audience remembers positively.

Having great stories and being enthusiastic, passionate, and entertaining is vital.

Getting the audience involved in activities during our presentation will take the entertainment factor to a new level. All of a sudden, the talk is all about them, and not about us, the speaker.

When they are busy being entertained, they do not have time to judge or have a negative attitude.

Every presentation we give can involve the audience.

How can we get them involved?

Having a series of activities throughout our talk will take the focus off us.

Activities, games and interactions help us get our point across through the audience's participation.

Talking **at** the audience does not work. Getting them involved does.

Exercises and activities.

Activities are effective because they can be linked to the goal of our talk.

Having an experiential element gives us a third dimension in any presentation.

The more senses we engage, the more they will remember our message.

They can see us.

They can hear us.

They can participate with us.

The point of any exercise is experiencing our message. If we rely on them to hear our message and act on it, it might not be enough if they were not listening intently. If we think they could see what we were trying to express with our body language and posture, we might miss the target if they were not looking all the time. Experiencing an exercise adds a layer that is multi-sensory. Speaking can be seen as one-way communication.

If we were financial planners, we might want to have the audience write down the amount of savings they have in the bank and then add 20%, because of how much more they'll make with what they learned from us. Then we can take them step by step through exercises to show how it's going to happen.

If we are selling a product, we want them to have a final experience of the product that is positive, so it's irresistible and they just have to buy it when you finish. That's when samples, product demonstrations and reminders of the benefits of the product are crucial.

If we wanted people to be more confident, they should do something to make them feel confident. This is how my public speaking workshops achieve their goal. The audience practices and demonstrates giving a speech confidently.

If we want to paint a picture of the future, we want them to put themselves into a future "dream" or "vision" so they see what they really want, and are inspired to act to make that dream a reality.

We can use many different ways to keep the audience engaged. We just need to have a range of options prepared. Then we can insert a relevant activity.

Simple activities can include:

- Encouraging them to raise their hand as a response to a question.
- Waving to them and getting the wave back.
- Applause to show recognition for participation.
- Laughing at jokes and at the responses people share to funny situations.
- Having the audience repeat what we say.
- Standing up to stretch and look around the room.
- Reflection and thinking time, with or without writing.
- Writing lists of goals, action steps, scripts or instructions.
- Creating a plan for finance, marketing or sales.
- Calculations of return on investment, savings, or the costs of a project.
- Handouts that require gaps to be filled in.
- Drawing a picture or designing an object like a car or house.
- Making a map to help someone find a shop, city or island.
- Partner activities to have conversations happening between audience members.
- Reviewing materials either provided to them or that are available online.
- Research into common myths and misconceptions.
- Roleplay to practice a skill or develop a talent.
- Discussing case studies to learn how things happened in the past.

- Strategizing in a small group or alone on how to grow a business.
- Competitions to encourage participation, problem-solving and achievement.
- Games that create a positive feeling amongst the group.

The activities.

In the exercises, we will use the following format at the beginning of each activity.

Length of time: This will range between one and five minutes.

Best time to use it: Some activities are better at the beginning, others in the middle, and others towards the end. Some are good any time.

Comfort zone scale: This is from 1 to 5. 1/5 is a real stretch and challenge for the audience, and 5/5 is very comfortable.

Humour: Is this activity likely to create laughter and a positive reaction?

Props and other items: Does the activity require anything beyond the audience's participation? For example, pen, paper, phone, partner, etc.

Five minutes.

Why is five minutes the longest ideal length of time for an activity?

Because it is long enough.

When we do an exercise, we are often tempted to allow more time than is needed.

Do they really need 15 minutes for a writing activity?

Does anyone meditate for 20 minutes in a workshop?

Can we keep an activity going for even 10 minutes?

Five minutes is a good rule of thumb as a maximum time limit for any activity.

Five minutes is a great way to use the power of time pressure to get results from our games and activities.

Most exercises, be they speaking, writing, partner, or physical, can be completed in five minutes.

Location, Location.

Length of time: One minute or less to research and use.
Best time to use it: At the beginning.
Comfort zone scale: 5/5. It is one of the first things in our talk.
Humour: No.
Props: Maybe, depending on the location.

The lights go down.

The audience applause finishes while we are walking up onto the stage.

"Good evening, Cleveland. Great to be back!"

Deathly silence.

Because you're in Pittsburgh.

The first thing every speaker needs to focus on is their location. It is even more important to pay attention if we are travelling around. Maybe we change cities every day. It is a sign of our preparation and professionalism when we mention the right location.

We tell our audience we know where we are because it is the fastest way to engage our audience and build rapport.

Fact: Everyone in the audience knows where they are.

Their city is important to them because they chose to live nearby, and come to listen to us speak today.

If it is true they work in the area, they may have gone to school and even been born there. Probably their parents and their friends and colleagues live there. So they will be proud of it, and everyone defends their home.

When is the best time to mention our location? At the beginning of our talk. Not in the middle, not at the end, but right up front.

"Thank you for that great welcome, Atlanta. It is great to be back in the home of Coca-Cola."

"Thank you for that introduction, Bill. Lovely to be back in Toronto, I'm looking forward to getting downtown to see the Blue Jays in action after we finish today."

"Thanks for having me here for my first-ever talk in Singapore. I understand that you live in a 'foodie' city and will have a lot of recommendations for dinner."

This will give us an advantage with our audience, as we already seem to know them. This makes them more comfortable. It will encourage them to lean forward and listen because you are already "local." It builds rapport and it builds trust.

How do we implement this beyond the examples above?

Be here now.

Where we were yesterday … the audience does not want to know. Where we are going next … they don't really care about.

Audiences will always compare themselves if we mention another town or city.

Does it mean we like it more?

Do we wish we were there?

Or maybe the people there are smarter, better-looking, and wealthier.

People are essentially insecure around strangers until they trust them.

If we mention where we are going next it looks like we cannot wait to leave.

If we live in the present, then focusing on the people in front of us will create the best outcome. Rapport, trust, and being liked all happen when we treat the audience in front of us as the most important audience we have ever spoken to.

Staying positive.

People will always defend if we attack. So it's a good idea to say only positive things about your location.

Imagine hearing a speaker say, "It's great to be here in New York. I was driving through New Jersey yesterday and I'm glad to be away from there!"

What if half the audience lives in New Jersey and came here to listen to us? We just alienated half the crowd. And probably upset the rest.

"Thank goodness I've left Chicago, the rain was so heavy and it was so windy!" This will not build rapport if we are at a national conference. What if a third of the conference audience is from Chicago? It would be ironic if it started raining right as we started speaking.

- If we talk at a high school, we do not talk about another nearby school.
- If you are a guest at a church - do not talk about how big another church is or how motivational their pastor is.
- Speaking to a hotel chain? Remember to use the name and location. Do not refer to a competitor that has more comfortable beds.
- We always talk positively about the speaker before us.
- When possible, say something positive about a speaker that follows us.

So let's look at the preparation we can do.

Visiting a new city?

Read a copy of the local paper online a day to a week before. See what the main issues are in the town.

Find out the name of the mayor. There are people in the audience who may engage when you mention the mayor's name. This shows we know where we are.

- Know a bit of history about the town or city.
- Find out who built it or settled there, and what made it grow. Industry, agriculture, tourism, etc.
- Identify some people from the town who became famous. Celebrities, movie stars, singers, and the like.

For bonus points, get a local person to give an introduction. Talk to them beforehand, and learn their name, their family situation. If you have more time, discover their goals, their job, and say nice things about them on the stage when you start.

Drink the water.

We should never appear afraid to drink the water unless a local tells you it is dangerous. We can also do research ahead of time. Do not comment in a way that could be seen as criticism of the people of that area. For example, Brisbane water had a lot of chlorine in it a number of years ago. In some hotels it still tastes the same due to the pipes and containers being infused with it. Locals are used to it and take offence if we make a comment about it.

Get into the food.

Try the local food specialty. If we speak in New England, we have to try clam chowder. Lucky enough to be in Naples, eat some pizza. In Texas? Get some barbecue. If we are at a conference in Thailand, eat a Pad Thai noodle dish from a street vendor. Loving local food is like loving the locals. Then we can reference it in our talk and see the audience nod, smile and like us.

Is it hot here?

If we say it's hot in Phoenix, Arizona at any time of the year, they will laugh at us. But they are used to it. And everyone is proud of what makes their city unique. Whether it is -15 degrees in Norway or windy in Chicago, it is unique to the location and accepted by the locals. Maybe it is a sandstorm in Dubai and you cannot see a metre in front of you.

A visitor cannot get angry at the weather, because the locals will defend it. They live there and deal with it every day and it is a part of their biorhythm. In Melbourne, Australia, there are sometimes four seasons in one day. It is a proud statement. But if a visitor comes to town and complains, they are regarded as rude. Then the audience - in a sales presentation or a conference presentation - will not engage with them like someone who comes and accepts it.

Speaking to a company?

- Know the company vision, mission, goals, and purpose.
- Know the name of the CEO.
- Know who invited you, who is introducing you, and who is paying you!
- What's the product range?
- Where does the company have offices? Just this one, or all over the place? Which one is the most successful?
- Is the company growing?
- How new is it - does it fit into the startup category?
- Are they traditional, with directors and investors, or did they use crowdfunding or philanthropy?
- If they are non-profit, are they a charity?

You can find all this out in a simple email to the person who brought you in to speak.

You need to work it into your presentation opening, as you say your "thank you" to the relevant parties. Then people feel acknowledged and valued and they lean forward and like you more.

What about a hotel?

- How old is the building?
- When did the hotel open?
- Who is the manager?
- How is the business doing? Just an opinion is enough.

- How many staff members does it have?
- Who is the main competitor?
- What makes them different?
- Are they admired or hated? Finding out the attitude means you can align rather than create a point of argument. If they respect their main competitor, you don't want to say "Let's crush the opposition!"

If the business is a startup, they are usually growing and making a name for themselves.

But you need to know so that you can tailor your message to growth and positivity. A message for a 50-year-old business is different from a message for a startup.

Speaking at a school?

- Who's the principal?
- How old is the school?
- How many students?
- How many teachers?
- Do they get a lot of funding, as a disadvantaged school?
- Or are they a private school with high fees?
- Is the surrounding area high, middle, or low-class?
- What year level are you speaking to, and how many kids? 10 is different than 100. You need different strategies.
- Is there a uniform?
- Is the school strict?
- Who is the favourite teacher?
- How successful is the school at getting kids into university?

- How successful are the sports teams?
- What else makes them unique?
- What other challenges do they have?

Speaking at a church?

- Who is the pastor/minister/priest?
- How many people attend/will be in the audience?
- What are the demographics?
- How wealthy are the attendees?
- What is the ethnic mix?
- Who is the most influential congregation member?
- When was the building constructed?
- How was that funded?
- What are the church's goals for growth?

These questions will give you a base to frame and shape the first impression you give when you start talking.

They help make the audience feel at ease, like you know them.

No one listens to strangers, but we do listen to friends, and people that "understand" us.

It's possible for us to listen to a total stranger because this principle is so powerful. It works. It's also possible for us to structure our talk to be that stranger who is an instantly-respected source of information.

Knowing enough about "where we are" is important. And it's why we have to focus on the audience and their surroundings even more than we focus on ourselves. When we do that, they feel like we care. And they will listen.

Once we meet a new person and have a conversation with them, we have a connection. It's like we have known each other forever. After a presentation, they should feel like they know us.

This should be by design. Not luck.

The better we understand the audience, the more a part of their life we are for that moment in time. The more they know us, the more they trust us. And when they trust us, there is a better chance that they will act on what we say.

The opposite is also true. If we do not build that relationship, we will be rejected and have poor results.

If a speaker comes to town for the first time, they want to sound local. Maybe they ask how to pronounce the name of the town but still get it wrong in their presentation. Then the crowd feels disappointed. Maybe when they speak they forget to mention the organiser. And they do not thank anyone for coming at the beginning or the end of the talk.

It doesn't matter how valuable the presentation is if we don't build and maintain rapport with the audience. It's going to be an uphill battle trying to get your message across.

Repeat business becomes easy. They will ask us to speak again if we seem like a friend. We will grow a customer and referral base. All this makes us more money and gives us more audiences to share our message with.

The Mirror.

Length of time: Less than a minute.
Best time to use it: Whenever we want the audience to come together as one.
Comfort zone scale: 3/5. We have to be the one to lead the audience into the activity.
Humour: Maybe.
Props: None.

What we see.

There are times when we look at the audience and think, "They do not look very receptive."

Whatever we are sending "out" to our audience, it will come back to us reflected exactly the same.

So if we see a bad audience, or sad faces, or people falling asleep, it is a reflection of what we are presenting to the audience.

Are the audience members leaning back in their seats, looking disinterested? Maybe it is time to increase our speed, volume and pitch.

Do they look angry? We need to get away from any negative focus and shift their attention to lighter, more positive topics.

If they are all leaning forward, taking notes, nodding, laughing on cue, it is good. The room will warm up with positive energy. It means something is working.

If we feel a connection to the audience, it feels great. It means they trust us. This feeling should inspire us to keep working hard and spend the time we need to get the same outcome again and again.

How do we use this to our advantage?

Leading the audience.

When we are giving our presentation, we will notice a high level of rapport when the audience starts to mirror our body language.

Anytime we want to have our audience doing something, we just do it first.

Here are a few things we can lead our audience with:

- Nodding.
- Clapping.
- Raising our arm.
- Dancing.
- Exercises like stretches or massages.
- Waving.
- Showing how big something is with our arms spread out.
- Energy levels.
- Speed of speaking.
- Pace of our walking.
- Jumping.

But how can we entertain them and have them participate?

Instruction.

The key to taking control of the entertainment aspect of our talk is to tell the audience what to do.

We need to give clear instructions on an activity or exercise.

We need to keep things on track and on time.

And we need to encourage the audience to copy our example in what we say and do.

If we instruct, we assume the power in the room and can encourage the audience as a collective to follow us. This creates respect from the audience, who will see that we have confidence in what we are saying.

When we stand up and stretch, we can ask everyone else to do the same. This activity is not accidental. It is always more powerful when everyone participates in the exercise. We just want to have an exercise or activity completed by everyone because it brings a synergy to the audience. And this helps us a lot in keeping the audience together and listening to us, a source of authority and power.

Just One Person.

Length of time: 2 minutes.
Best time to use it: Before we start talking.
Comfort zone scale: 5/5.
Humour: No.
Props: None.

We want to write our speech or talk and pretend like we are delivering it to one person.

We need to narrow our focus and start thinking about our delivery to the individuals in our audience.

People often say things about a speaker like:

- "She spoke to me."
- "I could really relate."
- "He made it easy for me to grasp the key concepts."
- "It was the right time for me to hear what she was saying."

We never hear statements like, "We all felt it was a great talk." It is a personal statement and a personal response.

- We want to believe that when the speaker says they can change our life - they are talking only to us.

- Prospects want to believe that when the speaker says they can create their own future, they mean them.

- The idealistic audience member believes it is them, when the speaker says, "Someone here is special."

How do we do this?

Every time we are writing a speech or sales presentation, assume there is only one person in the audience.

This will help us to write directly to the person we want to present to. It narrows the focus and laser-targets the perfect person to hear our message.

Prospects are individuals, not groups.

- On a video conference, we can usually only see ourselves, so we should present to ourselves as the single audience member.

- When we say "you," think of the ideal prospect listening.

- If we say "most people," we need to have statements that people will feel they can relate to.

- When we want to say something is possible, change it to "you can do it."

- Instead of saying some people will be successful, say "You will be successful."

- And when there is a group, do not fall into the trap of saying "Hello, everyone." Just say hello or good morning. Personalise your presentation.

- Instead of asking about **the** biggest problem, say "What is **your** biggest problem?"

- Instead of "Do we all know about the best insurance?" … say "Do you know about the best insurance for your needs?"

Speaking Activities.

Length of time: From one to five minutes.
Best time to use: Beginning and middle.
Comfort zone scale: 1/5 to 5/5. Many people do not like participating because their self-confidence is low. Others will jump right in. There will always be enough engagement.
Humour: Depends on the topic.
Props: None.

When we encourage the audience to talk, we notice a few things.

The energy level in the room goes up, as people compete to be the one speaking the loudest, the fastest, or with the most confidence.

The participation from the audience is 100%. After listening for a while, most people are bursting to say something to their partner or colleague, or simply wanting to hear their own voice.

When we allow people to speak, it releases the pressure that may have built up from just listening.

Speaking activities.

- In a team of five people, practice the opening sentence you like to use with prospects.

- In teams of three, practice the simple quick close asking for a decision on buying your product.
- With a partner, share your reasons for coming to this talk and answer any questions they have.
- Assuming you were coming on stage next, share the introduction you would like to have from the host or emcee.
- Form a group of 10 people and tell a story. One person says two words at a time, then the person on their right says two words, and so on.
- In a group of three people, discuss what you would do with $1,000,000.
- Nominate a spokesperson to present the findings of your group research.
- With a partner, share the story of how you felt about your teachers at school.
- In a group of five, share the values your parents had about money.
- Stand up one by one and share one goal you have this year.
- Stand up one by one and share the reason why you are here to learn about <insert topic>.

Want some more?

- Share something no one in the room knows.
- Count to ten in a foreign language you were taught when you were growing up.
- Find a partner and ask questions of each other, with every question to be answered with another question.
- Tell a story about an imaginary person going from rags to riches (poor to wealthy.)

- Share the amount of money you were paid per hour in your first job.
- Share how you made your first $100,000 in business.
- Share how you got your first sale.
- Share how you travelled to the presentation.
- Share something that you were afraid of as a child.
- Share the most positive quote you know.
- Whisper a sentence to the person beside you, and have them pass it on and on to 10 people.

The Blessed Silence.

Length of time: Three to five seconds.
Best time to use it: At key moments in our talk.
Comfort zone scale: 5/5. This is just planning.
Humour: Good timing of pauses in jokes can help.
Props: None.

Actors and actresses.

Nicole Kidman, a famous Australian actress, was being interviewed about an upcoming movie. Whilst beautiful and elegant in front of the camera, her "unrehearsed" presentation in the interview was poor.

She said "umm" a lot. About 11 times, every time she gave an answer to the interviewer. And she talked for 7 minutes. She seemed to "umm" instead of breathe.

This proves that without preparation, even highly-paid actresses can sound like amateurs. So what hope do we have?

The key is paying attention.

Nothing distracts an audience more than these filler words.

The words like "ummms", "aaahs", and "ohhhhs."

It could be "well," "so," "ok," "uh-huh," even "aaaaaand" or "and-um" during a speech.

Some speakers use the same filler words in every sentence, or to link sentences together.

We need to get rid of this bad habit.

We want to remove the distractions so our audience can focus on what we are saying.

Don't let the messenger get in the way of the message.

Opening our talk the same way every time becomes boring. When we use fillers like "ummm" and "ahhhh," it can sound unprofessional. It looks and sounds like we are disorganised. Maybe we will appear anxious or nervous. This will give our audience the wrong impression and affect the success of our talk.

We need to start listening to what we say. It is useful to watch video of our performances to see when we say certain things. This feedback helps us remove the bad habits and replace them with good ones.

When we remove unnecessary words, people will notice the improvement in our speech right away.

Why do we say these words?

1. People say "ummm" or "ahhh" between their sentences to avoid silence.

We have all heard people speaking like this. They finish a sentence with one breath, then "ummm," then move to the next sentence without stopping.

"Ladies and gentlemen, it is a pleasure to be here tonight ummmmm and I'm proud to be sharing with you the most important discovery in health you will ever hear about ummmm because it's the most dynamic ummmm and revolutionary product in the world ummmm and I have seen lots of products in the last 10 years so I know what I'm talking about."

Ummm.

Does that word annoy the audience members and distract from the material in the presentation? Of course it does.

2. People say "umm" because they expect to be interrupted.

Most people are used to being interrupted when they talk to friends and family.

But onstage, the audience respects the speaker. So they do not interrupt.

Learning to create a new belief that we can allow moments of silence will give our talk a strength it did not have before.

The audience will not interrupt us.

They might put their hand up for a question. They might even disagree, but they will respect our presentation until the time is right to engage in discussion.

Now that we know why we use these "filler" words, removing them creates space for something new.

Because we are the speaker, we have a hidden power we can use.

We can control the silence with pauses.

By planning when we pause, we can create the rhythm of our talk.

We can have times when we speak, as well as moments when we say nothing.

It is all about the timing. If we pause at the right time, it can have a powerful impact.

The pauses in our speech give it depth. A pause can give our audience time to think about the things we have said.

When to use a pause.

- After a key statement.
- At the end of a story.
- After telling a joke.
- After we have given an instruction.

Preparation.

Pauses, like all parts of our presentation, need to be prepared.

We need to write shorter sentences.

We need to use powerful phrases that will allow the audience to think about what we just said while we pause.

If we are writing a script, we can write the word "PAUSE."

Think of every pause as increasing the power we have on the stage. This should encourage us to pause more often.

And when we deliver this new and improved talk, our audience will be engaged. They will respond positively when they see how confidently we deliver our presentation.

Entertaining Stories.

Length of time: Up to five minutes.
Best time to use it: Before we start talking.
Comfort zone scale: 5/5.
Humour: No.
Props: None.

The best stories create an emotional response from the person listening. This in turn creates a strong memory for them. In the future, they will re-experience that emotion whenever they remember, hear, or tell the story.

The stronger the emotion, the longer the story memory will last.

What stories are the best to tell?

Our own.

Personal stories can be seen, heard and felt. A personal story told well is just like a movie. When we are watching a movie, we put ourselves in the role of the hero or the villain. We feel the emotions, we see the sunsets, and we experience the action.

When a good story is told well, it is a multi-sensory experience. It will be heard and seen and felt. This gives it greater entertainment value than a boring, unemotional set of facts or figures.

It is good to remember that the brain is a muscle. Muscles grow with use and they decay without it. In some research studies it has been shown that the creation of an emotional memory through repetition helps grow the brain. So the strength of the most important muscle we have depends on the emotions we experience.

Have we ever noticed someone who has no heart or feelings and we feel like they are "dead" inside? This is often the case. When the brain has not been stimulated enough with emotions and feelings in the formative years, there are side effects. People without emotional connections find it hard to build relationships and keep them.

It makes sense to give people memories that are strong and positive, and leave them with an experience they remember and want to repeat. We may be giving them the first positive emotions they have experienced in some time.

The best stories are about things that have happened to us. Our sharing of these experiences helps the audience engage their senses.

Good stories include parts of life that people can relate to. This is why biographical movies always have some "added" material so people remain interested. All this extra background information fills in the picture, and helps the audience feel like it could have been them starring in the movie.

Using our own life, how many stories do we have involving:

- Our father.
- Our mother.
- Our family.
- Our home.

- Our parents' careers.
- Our parents' values.
- Our parents' discipline.
- Our vacations as a child.
- How much money our family had when we were young.
- The dreams we had as a child.
- The isolation we felt as an only child.
- The responsibility we felt as an eldest child.
- Losing a family member, old or young.
- The sport we played when we were young.
- Our academic studies.
- Where we lived.
- Who we looked up to.
- What we wanted to be when we grew up.
- Our favourite vacation spot.

Now a lot of these may create story or movie themes that have a lot of drama in them. This is not always the point of our storytelling.

Some will have a lot of action and adventure.

Others may involve emotional moments and special, secret times not previously shared.

But unless we tie the story into our talk, we are just sharing a personal anecdote, and our audience will not get the link between the two.

So serious or dark stories always need to have a "silver lining" for every cloud. They need to resolve with a lesson, hope, or redemption.

Happy stories need to have a lesson or a metaphor for life and living.

Maybe we can look at these themes and tell a story about them.

- Competing for a prize.
- Finding true love in the most unusual place.
- Making a million dollars and donating it to charity.
- Finding a friend overseas to prove friendship is possible anywhere.
- Becoming confident enough to speak in public so we can inspire people with our message.

Let's look at some other themes.

- Our favourite subjects at school.
- Our favourite teacher.
- Our first job.
- The first time we kissed a girl/boy.
- How we got along with adults during our teenage years.
- The things at school we avoided.
- Musical instruments we played.
- Highlights of our school years.
- The worst thing that happened in our school years.
- Our relationship with religion.

These stories will give our audience an insight into our formative years.

When we are exploring our "firsts," we are in a period of discovery, as well as making mistakes and having small victories.

As we learn and grow, then we build habits for success which guide us into adulthood.

What stories can we tell next?

- The first thing we did after we finished high school.
- The places we travelled to after high school.
- The university we chose.
- The people we met at university.
- Choosing not to go to university.
- How people around us reacted to our decisions.
- The new influences when we became an adult.
- The first car we bought.
- Our first house away from our family home.
- The next love of our life.
- What became important, the shifting and shaping of our values.

Every stage of life has its own stories.

When we get stuck in our presentation and the audience is not looking entertained, we can use a story.

"Let me tell you a story."

"Have I told you about the time when I was five years old?"

"When I look back on my university years, this story gives me the motivation to be here with you today."

"What we are talking about here today reminds me of something my father used to say."

"When you look back on this talk, I want this story to stick with you."

Leading into our story will help the audience know that it is time to pay attention.

Using a story to entertain is a key strategy.

Having a good story is a key preparation strategy.

So do we need to write our stories into our notes?

Or will we remember them?

We need to prepare a list of the stories as we did in the last few pages. Be sure to have a range of stories that relate to the presentation.

If we are a salesperson, we probably do not need to share personal issues about our childhood bullying from bigger kids. But we may find there is value from sharing a story about being taught by our mother to respect every cent and only spend money where it provides good value.

If we are presenting network marketing business opportunities, our story about not having money when we were young may be interesting. But our story about another relative dying poor could be powerful.

How and when we tell these stories is important.

When is the best time?
Before the audience gets bored.

Visually, there is a lot to love about the process of entertaining our audience with stories. It means we can prepare by paying more attention to our body language. Our eye contact, our gestures, our body movement and our actions.

We need to bring our stories to life.

It is not just about the words.

With our actions, we can entertain by making the stories that we tell come alive. Help the audience to see them just like a movie.

Use stories from movies. Take *Jaws* for example, the classic shark movie.

If we tell the story of how big the wide-open mouth is, we will naturally hold our hands out wide.

Every fisherman knows that when you talk about a fish, your arms get wider and wider, till it almost looks impossibly big. Of course that's the one that got away.

What about when we talk about how we were feeling low? We move our body into a lower position. Get closer to the floor and look down.

When we share a story about the future, goals, hope and achievement, what do we do? We look up. We lift our arms. We make eye contact and nod to our audience. We have them reflect our words and emotions back to us.

Breaking the Ice.

Length of time: Two minutes.
Best time to use it: Before we start talking.
Comfort zone scale: 5/5. The people in the audience will love it.
Humour: Maybe, based on personalities.
Props: None.

Here is an interactive technique we can use before our talk begins.

Talking to as many members of the audience as possible before we begin is a strategic move. Anyone who has worked to get a seat in the front row will love being spoken to. We can find out their names, jobs and hobbies. We might even pose for a few quick photos.

It is important to get the permission of the people in the front row to interact with them personally. As individuals they like to be treated this way.

Maybe someone in the front row does not want to be there. Better to find out early, before you ask them to volunteer later and get a negative response.

There will probably be someone who loves to take photos.

And there is always someone who loves to volunteer.

Discover who is an enthusiastic talker. Encourage them to participate through the talk by asking questions, applauding, and laughing at our jokes.

We can use all this information when we get onstage.

Comedians do it all the time. They set up a joke, then generate scenarios using the audience to play the parts. Knowing the people in the front row helps us to get a better response throughout the presentation.

Trainers and teachers get to know their students. They have the benefit of learning about each person over time. The faster we get to know our crowd, the faster they will engage.

We need to find out who is in the audience BEFORE we speak.

So here is the checklist of what to do.

- Talk to the people in the front row.
- Introduce ourselves.
- Shake hands.
- Ask questions.
- Pose for a photo.

When we are giving our presentation, we can reference some of those people in the front row. Use them by personally referencing their story. Use their name, talk about their family, their goals and their dreams.

The audience then engages more and will interact. They will see the relationship growing with the speaker. The connection will be positive. All the signs will be there to show that the crowd is engaged. This includes the smiles, the nodding, the interaction and the laughter.

When that link is strong, it is much easier to get our message across. When it is weak, we will always feel like we are struggling to connect.

When the front row is excited and involved, the feeling becomes infectious. Everyone wants to have that positive feeling.

The key to remember is that it starts with us. We have to proactively communicate before our talk begins. Then, during the body of our presentation, there is a positive feeling and the talk is a success.

Keywords and Sound Bites.

What do we remember of the great speeches in history?

How long they went? How many points they covered?

Or the quotable passages? The "sound bites." The keywords people search for on YouTube and Google.

The phrases that are referenced again and again in the media and pop culture.

"I have a dream." These words by Martin Luther King, Jr. have been used repeatedly by speakers and presenters who want to motivate and inspire.

Politicians refer to the words spoken by politicians before them. "Ask not what your country can do for you, ask what you can do for your country."

Army commanders quote *The Art of War*: "If you know the enemy and know yourself, you need not fear the result of a hundred battles."

Many speakers, to encourage commitment and dedication, reference Winston Churchill's "Never, Never, Never ... Never Give Up."

Books.

In every great speech or presentation, there are phrases, sentences, and key words that we remember because they are well-known.

Our speech may not invent one phrase that everyone starts using. But you can use the same principle to get people focused on our material by using memorable key words and phrases.

Power phrases make the impact we want with our audience. They cut through the other things going on in their minds. We want them to sit up and pay attention to what we're saying, because we are interesting and entertaining.

Remember, entertaining presentations are providing value to the audience. And nothing is more entertaining than grabbing someone's attention and creating a memory.

When we are crafting our presentation, we want to have plenty of memorable keywords and phrases to deliver to our audience.

Then they will be forced to:

- Argue, discuss or disagree with what you have to say.
- Satisfy their curiosity.

Let's look at some power phrases, and why they create memorable, entertaining parts of our presentation.

"Change your life."

One of the most powerful phrases in the human language. It has the potential for transformation.

9 times out of 10, people will pay attention to these keywords. Even if for no other reason than they are hoping someone does have something that will change their life!

This phrase taps into one of our great needs, self-actualisation. Using our own time, talents and resources to make a difference in the world. Imagine if someone came back and said to us that our talk inspired them to go out and change the world!

If we have a valuable product or service we are promoting onstage, the chance is high that we believe it will change something for the better.

But we should not assume people believe in it as much as we do. Making this claim is going to be matched by our belief in the product or service. And because we talk with sincerity, our audience will believe us.

"When you drink this shake and lose weight immediately, you will feel that you have changed your life, never having to eat dry toast again to diet."

"Applying this skin cream will change your life. Look five years younger instantly, and in three weeks' time no one will recognise you."

"Making money is now easy. This business will give you an extra $170 per week and it will change your life. No more begging for money to go to the pub on Friday."

"Insurance does not have to be scary. Saving $500 and having peace of mind will change your life as you travel the world knowing that you are covered in every country you visit."

"If you get nothing else tonight ..."

Do people only need to get one thing from our talk? No, but we can encourage them to not worry about everything in our presentation. We want to encourage them to sit back and enjoy it. To be entertained.

"If you get nothing else tonight, you'll walk out of here with a greater confidence going onstage. You'll be a better audience member, and be clearer when critiquing other speakers about what works and what doesn't work, and why."

"If you get nothing else tonight, you will leave with a better knowledge of the mortgage loan possibilities available in the current marketplace."

"If you get nothing else tonight, you will have heard 5 stories of amazing skin transformations with the wonder product. And you can talk to those people at the end of the night to find out more."

"If you get nothing else tonight, you will have the template for creating an international business. The rest is up to you."

"People tell me this is the best part."

Here is another power phrase that speakers love to use. It brings into play one of the greatest marketing techniques. Highlighting the best part brings the attention of the audience back. And saying "people" means it is not just our personal opinion.

When we talk about ourselves, people don't believe as much as when others talk about us.

This is the power of the "third-party endorsement."

It might just be one of the most effective ways you can get the attention of your listeners. Why? Because someone else says this is the best part. They will lean a little closer to hear why it is a highlight. And in many cases they agree.

In e-books, certain sections can be highlighted. It is the "best part" principle at work. When 15 people highlight one sentence on a page, the next person reading seems to always choose the same sentence as their favourite. They do not highlight a single sentence beside it. They follow. If other people have seen this as the best part, it makes sense to agree and do it too.

"I have told you a lot about our product range. But customers tell me this is the best part of using these products: the lack of artificial colours and preservatives. The products are natural and they will feel natural."

"Our business has grown by 277% in the last 3 years. But the investors say the best part is that all the profits are being distributed every month, so you have constant cash flow."

"The value of this wonder drink for your health is proven by scientists. But the athletes using it say the best part is they will never fail a drug test due to the synergistic ingredient mix and FDA-approved quantities."

"For the first time, making money is easy. And parents say the best part is your children will see what you are doing, and be proud when they tell their friends what you do for a living because it gives them the lifestyle you always dreamed of."

With the right combination of words, we can create interesting statements the audience will remember. And if they remember them, they will tell other people about them long after the talk is finished.

Now, let's look at the power we have on the stage to lead our audience.

Questions?

Length of time: One minute per question.
Best time to use: Anytime.
Comfort zone scale: 5/5. It is something we do every day.
Humour: Not necessarily. Unless the question is totally irrelevant and comical.
Props: None.

Why do we ask questions?

- To involve the audience.
- To check in on the understanding of the audience.
- To test the mood of the audience.
- To encourage two-way interaction.
- To challenge beliefs.
- To check if people are awake.
- To give the audience a chance to participate in the talk.
- To get to the answer.
- To show the audience that you respect them and are asking, not just telling.
- To give you a moment to catch your breath.

Questions should hook the mind until the answer is given.

We need to grab the attention of the audience. Discover their hot buttons, their reasons for wanting to listen. And you need to do it throughout your talk.

Getting the audience engaged with questions.

Before we choose a question to ask the audience, we have to ask ourselves a question. What is the point of the question we are going to ask them? Do we know the purpose and the outcome we are looking for?

Does the question hook the audience's attention right away?

Good questions provide the chance to shed insight on our key topic or idea. They can also link to lessons we are learning.

What else is important about our questions?

Do our questions respect the audience's intelligence? We cannot assume anything, but we need to expect that the people listening to us have a standard level of understanding.

Do our questions lead to just a "yes" or "no?"

Yes or No.

Questions that get a "yes" or get a "no" are useful. Sometimes we want to generate a series of agreements or disagreements. The collective answers help to bond an audience together and help the presentation of our ideas.

The simple "yes" or "no" responses can create momentum in our presentation.

- Do you feel good about sharing your success?
- Are we all clear on the benefits of the skin cream?
- Can we move on to the next slide?
- Do you like the idea of an extra $1000 per week?
- Is this starting to make sense?

"Yes" answers are a great response our audience can give. It helps to show they are listening, engaged and interacting. And it gets them talking, not just thinking. When there is a verbal response, it helps to anchor the decision.

You don't always get the sale on the first "yes." Get a few more and the momentum will build towards the ultimate outcome.

"Do you want to waste your money?"

"No" is the obvious answer. And this answer often has some emotion in the verbal response.

We don't always need a "yes" to get to a positive outcome. There are some people that say negative responses from your audience lead to poor results. "No" is a great reminder to them of reality.

And if the audience is thinking "No," you should hear it from them. Thoughts lead to words. When your audience speaks out loud, the words become more powerful.

More questions about questions.

Do our questions challenge the audience? When we use this sort of question, it can be powerful for everyone in the room. We need a topic guaranteed to get a response from a challenge question. Especially if we want the audience to take action and change something significant in their life.

We can also use the challenge question to get people to make a decision. To commit to answering a problem, social issue or global topic.

Challenges are good if we look at key issues or philosophies in the news or current affairs. Maybe we are presenting an alternative point of view and want interaction with the audience. Maybe we just want to get them involved.

Need some ideas?

- Politics and leadership.
- Environmental issues.
- Immigration and refugees.
- Global poverty.
- Affordability of housing.
- Access to clean water.
- Global warming.
- Monopolies.
- Powdered milk in developing countries.
- Breastfeeding in public.
- War.
- Drug trade.

Do our questions seek to bring the audience into a conversation? Are we giving them the chance to take part by speaking, in an exercise or in writing?

Or are we just stirring the pot?

We need to have a purpose for our questions.

This is the problem with a Q&A session with the audience. No matter how hard we try, giving power to the audience means they can ask whatever they want. This may not let us continue in the right direction to make our point or get to our goals.

Inviting the audience to participate is always important if we want them to feel like they are in a conversation. They will not participate if they feel it is just a lecture. One key here is to not talk "at" the audience. This will prove to them that we do not want a conversation, we just want to tell them what to do or what to think.

Do they need time to think about their answer before we get them to share it with the rest of the room? Can we move on to a new topic before people have had a chance to share their answers out loud?

Can we ask questions simple enough for everyone to understand? We should not need to clarify our questions. They should be clear and easy for everyone to answer.

Simple questions to ask include the following:

- What do you think about <issue>?
- Where is our country/city/town headed in terms of environmental protections?
- Who will lead our country in 10 years' time?
- What is being done about the homeless crisis in Melbourne?
- Why do we have this obsession with other people's lives on social media?
- What will be different in your life this year compared to last year?
- How do we know you will do your part in reducing carbon emissions?

- What level of comfort will you have when you retire and stop working full-time?

- Do you have enough money to live for 20 years if you stopped working today?

- Who is responsible for your family's future?

- When did the world forget about manners in public?

- How many people have to die before they stop talking on the phone while driving?

- Do you know how many animals were used in the testing phase of this product?

- What is your country's response to the refugee crisis from <insert country>?

These questions challenge the audience and get them involved. The entertainment comes from the answers they give, and the way we handle them.

If we handle them well, the audience will respect us even more. And if we direct the questions in the right way, we can get a great outcome where everyone benefits.

Say It Again.

Length of time: One minute per use.
Best time to use: Throughout the talk.
Comfort zone scale: 5/5. It is simple to prepare.
Humour: Depends on the content.
Props: None.

Repeat.

One of the most inspirational speakers in history was the late Jim Rohn. Philosopher, mentor, speaker.

What made him unique and memorable? Why did people remember his speeches and key phrases? How did he get his message across so effectively?

When analysing his talks, something becomes very clear. Every time he would deliver a key phrase or sentence he would pause, then repeat it.

Word for word, as he built his presentation, the talk developed. When all the key phrases had been said at least five or six times, the talk was complete.

When reviewing his presentation we can see there were only 5 or 6 key phrases. But they had been repeated so many times that they were now embedded in the consciousness of the audience.

Repetition works.

And the important feedback was that people listening enjoyed the repetition. Not one person complained that it was too much.

"Before we start the day, plan the week. Before we start the week, plan the month. Before we start the month, plan the year!" This was a great talk. It had an impact that has affected millions of listeners. It defined a generation of time management seminars and trainings. People copied him a lot and discussed his content and style in many talks and books. Like we are doing here, in this book.

In the research, the word "plan" came up more than 100 times. Repetition works. It buries the message deep in the subconscious mind.

For the next week, the audience members would have the word "plan" sitting in the back of their minds. It was always being thought about even without them realising it.

- Every time we repeat our core idea or concept, more people notice it and will remember it.
- The more examples we share that tie back to the core idea, the better.
- The higher the number of times we say it out loud, the better our audience's retention.

Repetition helps us in the following ways:

- It reinforces the idea as being important.
- It helps to clarify the key idea of our talk.
- It gives a key focus point to come back to again and again throughout our talk.
- It helps us build on a simple concept.
- It helps the audience learn the lesson of an activity or game.

- It locks the focus of the audience.
- It can prioritise a topic.

What forms of repetition can we use?

Repeating our words.

"Plan the day, plan the week, plan the month, plan the year."

"Plan the day, plan the week, plan the month, plan the year."

Just repeat what we say at least once, making a precise and exact copy. This is useful for reinforcing a key point or sentence we want people to remember.

We can use this technique in the early part of our talk.

It might be good to suggest they write it down.

Give them time to write down the key sentence.

Pause and let it sink in. Then repeat it again.

Pause a bit longer, then repeat again. Then continue talking.

If it is a longer sentence, even one that is up on a slide or screen, repeat it again.

Warm up to it, give them warning that something important/key/vital is coming. And get them ready to write down this sentence.

This tells people that the direction our talk has been taking is leading to a focal point. When we get them to write something down, it will anchor it into their thoughts and into their notepad! And if something is important enough for the audience to write it down, they will.

When we present the key phrase the first time, wait 5 seconds before repeating it.

For example:

"Oh, this next phrase is so important, we'll want to write it down. Grab a pen, steal some paper, and engrave this into your memory forever."

(Pause)

"Never, never, never … never give up."

(Pause)

"I'll say it again, never give up. No matter what is happening to bring you down, never give up! When people around you say you should quit, never give up! When you think you have no energy left, never give up! It is always darkest before the dawn and it can be so hard to move forward, but … never give up!"

It looks strange when we write it down. When we say it out loud it is different. In fact, it is only a few words in a section of the talk. The repetition makes it memorable, and gives the key statement impact and increased value.

Take a moment and read that paragraph out loud, with pauses where each sentence stops. And feel the power in our voice, the energy it creates. The way we go up and down with our voice, and how that feels so different to just reading it on paper.

What are some of the other ways we can use repetition?

- We can do an exercise two or three times to improve our results.
- We can repeat case studies and examples to show our point.
- We can give examples.
- We can repeat a key word or phrase.
- We can repeat elements of our theme.

- We can repeat the name of a volunteer or person we are referencing.

- We should repeat the rules of any games or competitions we are running.

- We should explain how to solve a problem more than once.

- We should do everything at least twice if it is a demonstration.

Do not be afraid to repeat something important. This one repetition might be the key to the audience remembering it.

Reflection.

Length of time: Two minutes per variation.
Best time to use it: Early in a talk.
Comfort zone scale: 5/5. There is no necessary public sharing initially, so it gets more comfortable.
Humour: Yes.
Props: None.

Take the time to stop and reflect.

After outlining my first key point or strategy in a talk, I ask the audience to participate. They do this by having a two-minute period of reflection. I encourage them to have a pen and paper. To write down what they may already know, how they feel about the topic, and to consider any questions.

Reflection as an activity where you only use silence is not the point. There needs to be a focus for their time. A topic to think about. A concept to consider. Setting up the reflection time is easy, and can be done individually or in pairs.

Having a pen and paper, an iPad or a laptop can channel their thoughts into writing. And what they write in this time is often more valuable than the notes they take while we are speaking. This is because people cannot concentrate on more than one thing at a time. When they focus on their thoughts, memories, knowledge and ideas, it is easy to write them down clearly. When we ask them to write while we talk, it may be distracting.

Time is elastic.

This is a principle that I use in all time-sensitive presentations. Time is never running at the same speed. It depends on the context, the activity, and how busy our brains and bodies are.

What feels like a long time when you are speaking goes fast for the audience. But moments of silence when people are just thinking and reflecting? That period of time seems to take forever. This is good, because while they are reflecting, many thoughts can come to their minds which can be written down and reviewed later.

We can encourage people to share what they have reflected on. Or we can let them stay silent. There is always someone in the audience that likes to share.

We are also using a key principle in communication. The best presentations are always two-way. If the audience follows our instructions, they are interacting. Their writing, thinking and sharing gives them a chance to communicate back to us.

If we have created the opportunity for them to speak, then we can also respect what they say by listening. The value in the responses from the audience can be vital for us when we are working out what to say next.

What things can we get people to reflect on?

- Their financial situation.
- Their relationship situation.
- Their happiness.

- Their job satisfaction.
- Their goals for the coming year.
- Their achievements in the last year.
- The reasons they came to the talk.
- Their reasons for change.

Or if we are halfway through our talk, what to reflect on then?

- A question they would like to ask.
- What they disagree with so far.
- What extra information they need on the topic.
- What they have learned.
- What discoveries they have made.
- What information they would share with someone else.

At the end of a sales presentation, we can still use reflection.

- What will they do if they do not buy this product?
- What will happen if they keep doing the same thing?
- What will happen if they do nothing?
- What will be their financial situation if they stay in their job?
- What they want to earn in the coming year.
- Who they want to work with in the future.
- Where they want to travel next year on their vacation.
- What the most valuable part of the talk was.

Giving people time to think also helps them sell themselves. Because the motivation for change and making a decision comes from inside.

Silence and reflection really can be the best activity if we are not a professional closer, or we have given people deep concepts to think about.

Think for a moment about where it would be best in our talk. (See, it even works in a book.)

Summary.

Length of time: Three to five minutes.
Best time to use it: Middle and end.
Comfort zone scale: 5/5. It relies only on memory and is like speaking with just one person.
Humour: No.
Props: None.

Recap and review.

One effective activity that will help use up to five minutes of time is the strategic recap or review. This is the verbal version of the reflection activity, and the two can go side-by-side.

This makes the audience think. They can have the opportunity to talk about what they have heard. If there has been some value, they can review what they learned.

It helps the speaker to have the audience do a verbal review. Every time we talk about something, it reinforces the material presented.

They will remember more, and they will appreciate the chance to share their opinion with you and others.

Have the group form into pairs, threes or fours. They can spend five minutes discussing, summarising and reviewing the previous 15-30 minutes of the presentation.

Then, have a spokesperson from each group share with the audience; maybe what stood out most to them, or a point that they didn't agree with.

Our credibility is built as an expert and valuable speaker by the interaction from the crowd.

Shared learning provides its own connection between the groups and the individuals. The value to everyone in the room from sharing their discoveries and what was important is tangible. Because without the interaction, they would be relying on their own notes. But with collaboration, their learning and understanding increases. Many people enjoy listening to other people's experiences. They will write additional notes based on what other audience members are saying and get even more value.

This is a great activity to use in longer talks, at least an hour long. If we are speaking less than this amount of time, we should focus on delivery. Review can happen another time.

What are some good things to review?

- What we learned.
- What was the favourite part?
- What new ideas were generated?
- Where we see this information helping us?
- How to apply to our life?
- How to apply to our business?

When we stimulate our audience to think about what they have heard, they will come up with more.

- How our relationships will be affected.
- What we need to change.
- What challenges the talk brought up for us.

- What emotions we felt.
- The awareness of our skill level.
- Knowing how much we do not know about the topic.
- Personal reactions and responses.
- Negative emotions.
- Positive emotions.

All of these are good to review but none can be forced. This means that the process must be natural and organic.

If we can create this environment for the activity, the audience will help themselves, and feel like they are in control of a part of the talk. This bonds the audience to the speaker and helps maintain rapport.

Writing Activities.

Length of time: Two to five minutes per variation.
Best time to use it: Throughout a talk to reinforce creativity and problem-solving.
Comfort zone scale: 3/5. Low literacy levels could make this a bit uncomfortable. And other people only want to listen, not write. The value must be proven in the setup and debrief.
Humour: Maybe, but not necessary.
Props: None.

Got a pen, tablet or laptop?

Writing activities are easy to organise and manage. The audience can do about a page of writing in five minutes, so most of these activities work well to fill some time and get ideas out of their heads and onto paper.

Simple writing activities may be a word or sentence. But the act of writing is the key.

There are a lot of different writing activities we can do. Each writing activity can be chosen based on how long we want to spend doing it.

Writing is good because it carries an instruction from the speaker into something tangible. The words on paper are kept by the audience long after the talk is finished. And with a good tie-in to our topic, the writing can reinforce a point, or help the audience make a discovery.

This can be useful if we are selling something and want them to write down the benefits.

Or to outline a problem, highlight some pain and provide a solution.

Maybe the simple writing or calculations will help them sell themselves.

Or writing a letter or speech can be the foundation of change.

If we remember the key tool of instruction, we can get our audience to participate in even the most challenging activity. The best case scenario is a sheet of paper with writing on it. The worst case is they at least think about it, even if they cannot even write one word.

What are some things we can write about?

Lists.

Lists are easy because they are not long sentences. Just individual items. They are a great introductory writing activity.

- Write a list of your closest 20 friends.
- Write a list of your favourite foods.
- Write a list of the people you want to talk to when you're successful.
- Write a list of the places you want to go on holiday in the next 5 years.
- Write a list of the jobs you wanted to do when you were young.
- Write a list of business names that could represent you.

- Write a list of the websites that you visit the most.
- Write a list of the apps you use the most on your phone.
- Write a list of numbers in a foreign language.

Names.

We all know people. We can pull the names of people or things from our memory, or our dreams and goals.

- Write down the name of the first book you would like to author.
- Write the names of the actors you'd like to be in a movie with.
- Write the names of the teachers from your childhood school.
- Write the names of the brands of clothing you wear at the moment.
- Write the names of as many countries as you can.
- Write the names of as many capital cities as you can.
- Write the names of as many music artists as you can.
- Write the names of as many personal development speakers as you can.
- Write the names of your favourite authors.
- Write the name of the island you want to visit next.
- Write the name of your favourite city in the world, even if you have never been there.

Top Five.

For great entertainment when sharing with the group after the exercise, a top five list narrows the audience's focus.

- Write the top five principles you were taught about money as a child.
- Write the names of the five most influential people in your life.
- Write down five secrets to a successful relationship.
- Write five keys to building a business online.
- Write down five marketing ideas no one else is using.
- Write the best five slogans you remember from advertising.
- Write your five favourite ice cream flavours.
- Write the names of the top five CDs in your collection.

Writing exercises provide the audience with a permanent record of their participation and engagement in the talk.

When we have them share some of these things in a speaking activity, we get even more involvement.

More Writing Activities.

Three types of writing activities described here include a speech, a letter, or a plan. Each requires a dedicated amount of time to get started with a minimum duration time of five minutes. The draft created in that time can then be discussed in the group. Or it can be used as a springboard for more writing either during the talk or when they have gone home.

Speeches.

Speeches should always have a few drafts before we perform them. Even if we do not read them out word-for-word, we will need to practice first. Each draft we edit makes the talk better and better. And after reading it out loud three or four times, we may have it memorised.

- Write a one-page introduction of your mother.
- Write a one-page introduction of your father.
- Write a one-page introduction of yourself.
- Write your Academy Award acceptance speech.
- Write your Grammy Award acceptance speech.
- Write your MTV Awards acceptance speech.
- Write a wedding speech as the bride, groom, father of the bride, or best man/maid of honor.
- Write a Presidential acceptance speech.

- Write a speech for your favourite cause.

- Write a speech that shares your secrets of success.

- Write a speech about what you learned in high school.

- Write a speech about what you learned from being a mother or father.

- Write a speech about how your life has changed from when you were a teenager.

Letters.

A letter is a very personal document. It can still be drafted and edited like a speech. However it will read more like a direct message. Its goal is for one person to receive it and read it to themselves. This is a powerful activity as it can be quite emotional.

- Write a letter to your 5-year-old self.

- Write a letter to your grandchildren.

- Write a letter to your parents.

- Write a letter to anyone who hurt you when you were young.

- Write a letter to the prime minister or president of your country.

- Write a letter to your future self.

- Write a letter to your high school counsellor.

- Write a letter to God.

- Write a letter to people who said you would never make it.

- Write a letter to your last boyfriend/girlfriend.

- Write a letter to your ex-wife/husband.

- Write a letter to someone you have a crush on.

Plans.

Plans never happen by themselves. They are constructed, modified and adjusted many times. But the "plan" for a plan is the same. Start writing some ideas about what needs to happen.

In a business or marketing plan, there are templates we can use. The key is to find out what you think you need to accomplish. Then fill in the gaps with what has to be done to get there. And then find the way to make that happen, based on the resources and budget and time available.

- Write a business plan for your new business idea.
- Write a marketing plan to launch the new product being discussed in the speech.
- Write an action plan for sponsoring more distributors.
- Write a reading plan for the books you want to read this year.
- Write a personal development plan for the books, CDs and seminars you need to invest in.
- Write a professional development plan for the networking, training and certifications you need.
- Write a financial plan to present to the bank for remortgaging your house so you can invest in a franchise.
- Write a financial budget for your household for the next month.
- Write a plan for the publishing of your first book.
- Write a plan for the emergency evacuation in your workplace.
- Write a plan for getting out and dating again.
- Write a plan for your online marketing strategy.

- Write a plan for your word-of-mouth marketing strategy.
- Write a plan for the purchase of a new home this year.
- Write a plan for a promotion at work.

Five minutes will never be enough to perfect any of these activities. But it is a good start. And when people start, they can look later and see there is something to build on.

Mission Statements, Goals and Plans.

Length of time: Five minutes for each draft.
Best time to use it: After setting up the importance of a mission statement, purpose statement, goal or plan.
Comfort zone scale: 5/5. Everyone can express their personal values in a statement.
Humour: No.
Props: None.

Longer writing activities.

Writing out a mission or vision statement can be a key to achieving transformation in the audience.

When we talk about how important it is, the next natural step is to have them write something.

Like all writing activities, it does not have to be perfect. But it is important to start.

Writing a personal statement or a company mission is intense work. So is writing out a list of goals for the coming year.

It is a great activity to get people away from theory and into the practical application of what has been shared.

If we talk about a one-year goal plan, then five minutes to write a list of ten to fifteen goals is plenty of time.

If we talk about a two-year business plan, then five minutes will only provide an outline. The full plan may take three hours back at the office or at home.

If we want to write a mission statement or statement of purpose, this can be drafted within five minutes. Then the group can share their results, and add to the document in round two of writing.

How do we run the activity?

Ask the audience to get a piece of paper or their iPad/laptop and attempt a draft. Just the skeleton or bare bones of a document they will work on later after the talk.

When we give them five minutes to do the activity, it will go very quickly. But this is a key part of the process of beginning something new.

When we start, we have something to work with.

If we only have the theory, it is much harder to start when we get home.

Drawing.

Length of time: Five minutes or more.
Best time to use it: Middle of the talk.
Comfort zone scale: 5/5. Even if they don't draw well, everyone can participate.
Humour: Depends on what they draw.
Props: Pen, paper, iPad, laptop, flipchart, screen.

Not everyone likes to speak.

Some people love writing, and others drawing, sketching or painting.

Others like to work with wood as a carpenter, others with stone as a sculptor.

We cannot do every creative arts activity in our talk, but sometimes a drawing can be powerful. It can be shown in the front of the room. Maybe if they like it they can take a photo that is put onto social media sites.

Drawing can be a simple way to express things instead of writing. Good writing is hard, but a picture can be worth a thousand words.

- Draw a picture to describe your life so far.
- Draw a picture of the life you are trying to create.
- Draw a picture of how you feel about money.

- Draw a picture of the things you like to do in your spare time.
- Sketch the face that represents your ideal partner.
- Sketch a landscape including a beach, trees and hotels in the background.
- Sketch the perfect smart phone.
- Sketch the ideal vehicle of the future.
- Sketch how a city would look from above if you designed it.

We can also draw:

- A map.
- Ourselves.
- Our family.
- Our current home and our ideal home.
- What happiness means to us.
- What success looks like.
- What being poor looks like.
- An object or animal that represents us in the Western or Chinese zodiac.
- The journey of our life along a timeline.
- A hotel.
- An island.
- A concept or idea for a car, plane or rocket.
- A treasure map.
- A mind map for our future.
- A graph of our personal savings over time since graduating high school.
- Almost anything.

The point of a drawing activity is to get away from people taking information through their eyes and ears. Instead, we get them focusing on pouring their thoughts and feelings out into images.

What if people cannot draw?

This is a good point. Many people cannot draw, just like many do not like reading or speaking out loud.

Have the flexibility to allow people to write or orally describe what they want to draw.

Or in a goal-setting workshop or visually stimulating training, use magazines and newspapers. Let them cut out pictures to represent the things they want to draw.

Numbers.

Length of time: One minute or more.
Best time to use it: Throughout the talk.
Comfort zone scale: 5/5. Simple numbers that everyone can work with.
Humour: No.
Props: Not necessary, but a pen and paper or phone to write them down may be useful if the numbers are referenced later.

1, 10, 100.

Using numbers in our presentation is a great form of activity because it gets people working on something that will create a result.

When we have to focus on numbers, it brings back memories of school and mathematics classes. Not everyone enjoys that. So it is important to do these activities in a group where possible.

How can numbers be part of an entertaining and engaging activity?

The only forms of math that were any fun when we were young were simple things like addition and subtraction, multiplication and division.

Not calculus, trigonometry, and statistics.

So we need to do exercises that tap into the playful nature of a 6- or 7-year-old.

Do activities that include simple addition.

Do activities that have basic whole numbers.

Relate numbers to money. That is always exciting to add up money to show what we can make.

How else can numbers be used in activities?

- Counting.
- Doubling.
- Random statistics like 75% of Iran's population is under the age of 30.
- Key numbers like 3/10 people will get to 65 years of age with less than $1000 in the bank.
- Working out how long things take in years or decades - e.g. working for a boss.
- Using actual numbers as a frame of reference, like how much credit card debt the audience has.
- Working out a balance sheet of assets vs. liabilities.
- Calculating interest rates.
- Showing the return on investment of a deal.
- Showing the profit in a deal.
- Showing the value of a product.
- How efficient a product is - e.g. cars, miles/gallon or litres/km.

Numbers are good "sound bites" that people will remember and reference later on in the day or days following the presentation.

Partner Activities.

Length of time: Five minutes.
Best time to use it: Early in a talk.
Comfort zone scale: 1/5-3/5. Depends on if one or both people are shy. Or are strangers.
Humour: Most of the time people find something funny about each other or their responses in the activities.
Props: Sometimes.

More fun with a friend.

It is more interesting doing an activity with at least one partner. Treating the room as individuals is important, but the dynamics of a group come into play with at least one partner. Two or three can be even better.

Using a partner creates a buzz in the room. That buzz can produce an infectious enthusiasm. When doing a partner activity, the audience relaxes. They can talk, and they can get extra senses involved.

"Please select a partner." Who?

- The person beside you.
- The person behind you.
- The person who is about as tall as you.
- The person opposite to you.
- The person with same colour shirt.

- The person with same phone as you.
- Someone in the room who has the same hairstyle.
- Someone with the same brand of jeans on.
- Someone wearing a tie (or not wearing a tie).

Having a partner helps to get the audience talking to people around them. Many times the audiences are all strangers. This can help to break the ice. When they know each other, the activities can be even more powerful, as they push each other to participate and engage.

The learning effect of a shared experience is multiplied.

This partner may be a stranger or a colleague or a friend. Regardless, both people should participate in the activity. This is a key point, because if only one person does the activity, the power balance is out. Sharing the experience gives more than twice the learning when both participate.

Everyone benefits when everyone does the activity.

While people are choosing a partner, it gives us a moment to gather our thoughts ahead of the activity we are going to do. Maybe have a glass of water. Take a few deep breaths, or stretch our fingers or review our notes.

There are many activities you can get people doing with a partner.

- Reviewing material.
- Research.
- Roleplay.
- Discussing case studies or examples.
- Strategising.
- Competitions.
- Games.

- Laughing.
- Using their phones.
- Skill practice.
- Speaking in public.
- Designing.
- Planning.

Do we change partners? Not all the time. Just when we feel the first pair or group has spent enough time together, and it is more valuable to mix people up with new ones.

Competitions.

Length of time: Five to fifteen minutes, depending on the number of repetitions.
Best time to use it: Early in a talk.
Comfort zone scale: 1/5-3/5, depending on how competitive people are.
Humour: Depends on the activity.
Props: Specific to each competition.

Winners and losers.

One of the most effective ways to entertain our audience is to run competitions. Just listening and taking notes is boring.

For example, imagine we are sitting in a workshop. Someone asks us to write down the names of three places we would love to travel.

Most of us can do that. But so what?

The way to make this a more engaging activity, and to guarantee it is completed, is to turn it into a competition.

The only thing we need to add as the workshop facilitator or speaker is the following:

"I'd like you to make a list of all the vacation spots you'd like to visit. I'm going to give you five minutes. The person with the most spots will win a prize. Here are a few suggestions: Vegas, Paris, Jamaica. Write the city or country. And in five minutes, if you write quickly, you should be able to get 40 or 50! Ready? Your time starts … now!"

This gets people excited.

First, that they can open their minds to having multiple vacations.

Second, a prize brings out the competitive spirit. Some personality types know they have a chance to win, while others give up right away. But the results of the exercise will always create a positive energy in the room.

At the end of the time limit, ask for the total number of spots people wrote down. Everyone should have at least three. Then the competitive individuals show up with 10, 20, 50 or more.

We can get the final 5-10 people to stand up. Applause all round. Some words about competition, creativity, and desire. Then get to the winner and that magical number. More applause.

The activity does not end there. We put everyone into pairs or small groups and ask them to share their lists. And when they hear somewhere new, they can add to their lists. Because there are no rules saying we cannot. The more, the better.

This helps everyone dream bigger dreams and have bigger goals.

What other competitions can we run?

The hunt for volunteers.

Ask for a volunteer to answer a question. Then reward them with a prize.

Ask another person. Give another prize.

Now the audience is conditioned to answer questions, with the expectation of a prize.

The competition becomes … who can volunteer the fastest.

People will volunteer for the duration of our talk, and we continue to reward them with applause and prizes.

Writing long lists.

- Names of foods.
- Cities in the world.
- Careers.
- Ice cream flavours.
- Clothing brands.
- Car models.
- Hotel chains.
- Islands.
- Countries.
- Girls' names starting with S.
- Dog breeds.

Rock, paper, scissors.

This gets the entire audience involved in a game of pairs. With music playing and a lot of positive energy, the competition continues. Then there are just two people playing off in the grand finale. Issue a prize.

How to run it?

Form pairs, and winners choose another winner to battle. But the energy comes from the losers cheering on the person that beat them. And so on, and so on.

This is a noisy exercise. There is a lot of buzz in the room and will be applause and cheering all around for the winner.

Prize? The title of champion. Maybe an acceptance speech explaining how they did it on stage. This is a lot of fun and great to bring the energy up in the room.

Tell a joke.

The same elimination concept can be used from the last game. Perfect in a room of 20 to 200 people.

Everyone thinks up a joke or funny story less than 30 seconds long. They find a partner and tell it to them. Funniest joke continues. No one changes their joke, they just keep playing off against other people. The eventual winner presents the joke onstage to everyone.

Prize? A video of them delivering their joke in front of a live audience who already thinks the joke is funny. Maybe we kickstart their comedy career.

Team competitions.

Forming a team helps create healthy rivalry within the room. We can create teams by numbering people off or segmenting the room. Maybe we can choose captains and let them build a team.

Teams can compete in all sorts of competitions.

- Trivia quizzes.
- Dancing.
- Presentation of a new idea.
- Constructing something and being judged on its appearance.
- Singing a song.
- Writing a speech.

- Creating an entertainment item at a retreat or camp.
- Building a fire.
- Making a boat to cross a river.
- Building a human pyramid.

Volunteers.

Length of time: Five minutes per exercise.
Best time to use: Early and middle.
Comfort zone scale: 1/5-5/5. Depends on if they want to volunteer or not.
Humour: Created by the volunteers or their actions.
Props: Microphone, chair and the volunteer.

Can I get a volunteer?

The best engagement a speaker can create is getting volunteers - the proactive decision to be involved in the presentation by a member of the audience.

Volunteers are the best example of the speaker being liked by someone in the audience. Volunteers want to succeed more than most. They also like to be the centre of attention.

Want an example?

At the beginning of a public speaking workshop, everyone is involved. They share their experiences by standing up and speaking.

Later in the workshop, people are given the chance to come onto the stage, in front of everyone, to share what they have learned. They are handed the microphone and everyone is excited to listen. They are more attentive to the volunteer than the speaker.

Long after the opening of the workshop where everyone is nervous, now the volunteers appear confident and experienced.

A volunteer shows everyone in the room what is possible. Someone can start out shy and completely unwilling to speak in front of anyone. Then we see them speaking onstage just a few hours later in front of dozens or even hundreds of people.

After a workshop in the Netherlands recently, someone sent an email saying how much they wished they had gone onstage. They realised that the personal growth from the experience would have helped them in many ways. And they committed to volunteer more in the future. They were grateful that someone else volunteered because they saw what was possible. This was a key benefit they worked out for themselves.

There are always people who will want to volunteer to come up onstage. These are the people who want to get involved. Front-row people are always willing to get involved and interact. In an audience of strangers, this makes it even more important to get to know the people in the front row before our talk.

Involving a volunteer gives the audience "one of them" on the stage. Now the student becomes part of the teaching. The audience member becomes the performer for a brief moment. This person is now a part of the action and a vital part of the presentation. The volunteer will help to shape the memories people have of this day. And even though 80% of the audience will never volunteer, many will wish it is them up on the stage. They think of what they would have done differently. They even hear themselves speaking and get to experience the talk from a new perspective.

Getting to know the audience before we open our talk is a good idea. Volunteers identify themselves quickly. They often talk about the last time they were a volunteer. They mention the talk, the training, the speaker or the location. That will help us when the time comes to choose someone.

We want the volunteer to succeed when they come on the stage. We want them to perform the task we have set for them and improve with some of our training and coaching. Or perhaps we have a skill they can practice right there and then.

Sometimes the volunteer has the ability to inspire the rest of the room. It sets a great example to take action, after they stepped out of their comfort zone and tried something new.

What about some ways we can get the audience to volunteer?

- Answer a question.
- Do a roleplay on the stage.
- Research something on their phone.
- Record a video.
- Take a picture.
- Be hypnotised.
- Practice a speech.
- Write on a board.
- Act out a scenario.
- Build something from Legos.
- Tell a story.
- Do a magic trick.
- Mimic our movements.
- Try a product.

- Do a physical exercise activity like push-ups.

Something more ambitious?

- Have them read out a speech.
- Sing a song.
- Perform a dance.
- Lead the audience in an activity.
- Tell a joke.
- Solve a puzzle.

Volunteers are used to getting a positive result in the entertainment we are providing. They should not be negative. Volunteers should never fail, even if they do not perform an activity correctly.

How do we prevent this from happening? Can we save someone's ego if the volunteering performance is a disaster?

Of course we can. We set the audience up so no matter what, the volunteer is thanked.

The audience claps when they come onstage. And they will clap no matter what the result. Because the people sitting down are always willing to acknowledge someone with courage. And volunteering takes courage.

Role Play.

Length of time: Five minutes. Can be repeated for up to fifteen minutes.
Best time to use: Middle.
Comfort zone scale: 1/5-5/5. Some people are born actors. Others may not love the spotlight.
Humour: Sometimes. Yes if people are nervous and trying something new. Not if they become bored with the role play or feel it is not challenging enough.
Props: Sometimes.

Practice before the real world.

In the training world, we use role play to simulate a real-world situation; to practice a scenario and test our ability to manage it.

For example:

"You are a victim of crime. Please tell your partner, who is a police officer, what happened. Partner, you are to practice active listening."

This puts two people together, and in the scenario they can "act" the parts given to them.

The important part of any role play is the setup and the debriefing. When those are managed well, the audience will feel there is value in the activity.

The setup takes a while to do. We need to make sure everyone knows what we will be doing and what our intention is.

The debriefing is even more important. We have to go through every outcome the audience experienced. Then we can move forward onto the next example.

If we want to present a scenario that is unfamiliar, the role play may be difficult. So the setup is more important than ever. We have to give them a reason to push their comfort zone and do something that may feel unnatural and weird.

"You are a blind person and need to be helped through a busy intersection. With a partner you are to answer their questions to get where you need to go.

The scenario is confronting. The setup is clear, but it presents challenges. Illness, disability, age and race all can create barriers.

We can discuss the type of questions required with the audience before commencing the activity.

Then after everyone has had the experience of the exercise, debrief the activity by asking questions like:

- "How did it feel being blind?"
- "How did it feel answering questions?"
- "How did it feel offering help?"

And so on.

Get feedback from as many people as possible before moving on.

Role play scenarios should be done at least 3 times. The first time is often uncomfortable. But like everything, the more we do it the easier it becomes. With small variations each time, the role play can become more complex. This will encourage more participation and longer discussions in the setup and the debriefing part of the activity.

What are some other topics for role play?

- Relationship issues.
- Rehearsing a sales presentation.
- Telling a story.
- Managing a human resources issue at work.
- Firing someone.
- Interviewing a prospect.
- Meeting a lawyer.
- Breaking up with a partner.
- Talking to a child.
- Disciplining a teenager.
- Reading out loud.
- Practicing a speech.
- Creating an introduction.
- Outlining a business plan.
- Presenting to a banker.
- Sharing our feelings with our partner.
- Breaking bad news.

Shaking Hands.

Length of time: One to two minutes per variation.
Best time to use it: Early.
Comfort zone scale: 5/5 - we do it every day. It is easy.
Humour: Yes. The awkward nature may result in nervous laughter.
Props: None.

"Good to meet you."

The best part of this activity is the number of varieties we can use.

When we get the audience shaking hands with each other, it helps to break the ice. It may get the audience talking with each other and interacting with the speaker.

To add an extra twist to this exercise, try the following variations.

Ask the audience to stand up and choose a partner.

- Then ask them to shake that person's hand, but using their left hand instead of their right.
- Ask them to shake hands, with one person using their left hand, and one using their right.

- Ask them to turn around and shake hands with the person beside them, but one of them closes their eyes first.
- Ask them to shake hands using both hands, one over the other.
- Ask them to shake hands without smiling or making eye contact.

All create different reactions from the audience, some of which can be entertaining.

They change their way of doing an everyday habitual greeting. It can feel weird, and challenge the traditional ways of doing anything.

This is what makes the process interesting, and we can then talk about it in the debriefing part of the exercise.

When done correctly, the activity is a great metaphor. It shows it is possible to do new things, create new habits. It may even encourage the participants to look outside the usual ways of doing things. This breeds innovation and creativity.

What other ways can we shake hands?

- Close our eyes and shake hands. We can use our other senses to guide us.
- Shake our right hand with their left hand or vice-versa. Using the opposite hand helps us to feel uncomfortable in a new situation, but we can still succeed at the task.
- Shake with both our left and our right. Double-handed handshakes can be a lesson in intimacy. The "invasion" into someone's personal space may create discussion and emotional triggers.

- Shake shoulders, not hands. Put your hand to their shoulder and greet them. This brings eye contact into play and may create a more intense feeling.

- Shake hands backwards. Stand back to back and then reach for our partner's hand. The awkwardness can be a symptom of what it is like when two people meet on a date for the first time.

- Shake hands in the sports style - wrapping around the thumb with the elbow bent. This strong position often turns into a chest bump or hug with a pat on the back. See what instincts take over and where we are willing to end.

Every activity needs to have a purpose. When we apply the lesson to the activity, it creates a memory for the audience they can reflect on later.

Do not just tell. Demonstrate, get participation, debrief, and the exercise will have been valuable.

How to Spend
a Million Dollars.

Length of time: Five minutes.
Best time to use it: Anytime.
Comfort zone scale: 5/5. No pressure, and the list is personal, which motivates them to complete it.
Humour: From a few people in the audience.
Props: Pen and paper/phone to write.

This activity is easy to set up.

Ask the audience to get a piece of paper or their phone.

Ask them to write down the number "one million."

But not in words, in numbers.

1,000,000.

Then get them to think for five minutes about how they would spend that amount of money.

Ask them to write down their answers. Then share them with a partner. Then share them with the rest of the audience (the interesting ones).

This exercise can be humorous and it can be difficult getting the answer out of people. Or it can provide amazing investment alternatives the audience has never heard before.

How we spend our money says a lot about our habits, our values, and our creativity.

What happens next?

Most people start by writing about paying off bills. Then they move to taking dream vacations, and buying gifts for family and friends. Maybe they pay off a mortgage, car, or consider buying a bigger house for themselves or the people they care about.

But most people get stuck after a while and cannot spend the money.

Other people in a better financial position will have a range of investments they will put the money in. It is not as emotional for them because they already have a strategy.

When the audience shares their answers, we see how people value money differently. We can all learn from each other.

What are some of the ways people can spend the money, in case we need to give them a prompt?

- Harley-Davidson.
- Trans-Siberian Express train journey.
- Antarctica boat voyage to see the penguins from "Happy Feet."
- Paying off the family home.
- Paying off tax debts.
- Paying our families' debts.
- Buying new furniture.
- Putting the children into private school.
- Taking the children out of school and travelling the world for a year.
- Building a new home.

- Buying land.
- Buying a franchise (or two).
- Quitting our job.
- Starting a business.
- Updating our wardrobe.
- Updating our husband's wardrobe.
- Renovating the family home.
- Buying a boat.
- Opening a restaurant.
- Making a large donation to charity.

Most people run out of things to buy sooner or later. Unless they buy a million-dollar yacht or a mansion.

Showing them that there are activities they could now do if they didn't have bills or a job creates a whole new list.

- Attending conferences and seminars.
- Buying a lot of books.
- Going back to university.
- Studying for an MBA.
- Writing a book.
- Going on a retreat.
- Studying Veganism.
- Learning to play the piano.
- Starting to paint.
- Becoming a mentor.
- Having more children.
- Volunteering for a favourite charity.
- Taking a year off work.
- Learning a new language.

Many of these things we could do anyway. The concept of having $1,000,000 opens up everyone's creativity. Because money and security issues are removed, we feel a freedom to do things for ourselves.

This is a great activity in a workshop or seminar on prosperity or abundance thinking.

It also helps clarify people's priorities in the charity or non-profit sector.

This would fit into a talk on lifestyle, business development, or network marketing.

It can also be timely in an investment seminar when we are offering reasons to work hard now. Work hard now, to get the rewards later.

Tie the $1,000,000 to an action they can take or a mindset shift they can make. Then they can see what is possible for them, and commit to it in the moment right now.

Handouts.

Length of time: Two to five minutes per variation.
Best time to use it: Early in a talk.
Comfort zone scale: 5/5. Unless there are literacy issues, handouts are tangible, physical and cannot be ignored. Easy to use.
Humour: Yes.
Props: None.

Please pass these out.

Every presentation can benefit by handing out something to the audience. They can hold it in their hands. They can look at it. All of these are positive options. After all, if they are holding a sheet, they are not on their phones.

Paper handouts should be at least the size of a full sheet of paper, big enough to cover their notepad. If it is a sales sheet or order form, we want that in their peripheral vision while we speak.

As our talk continues, our value increases. Then the desire to get more of anything we are offering increases.

Handouts can also be great when they are interactive, even when they are as simple as filling out a form. This engages the sense of sight and touch. It also engages sound of course, as we instruct people how to fill it out.

Sample handouts to stimulate the creative mind include:

- An order form - for what you're selling that day.
- A newspaper clipping.
- Strategy or planning documents.
- A business plan template.
- A marketing plan template.
- A crossword puzzle.
- A coupon.
- A piece of paper to put an email address on.
- A training workbook.
- An instruction manual for using a piece of equipment.
- A photograph of a key object or idea in your presentation.
- A map.
- A story.
- A comic strip.
- A newspaper.
- A mystery object.
- A piece of costume jewelry.
- A fossil.
- A pen.
- A receipt.
- An invoice.
- A bill for utilities.
- A photo.
- A part of a machine.
- The foreword of a book.

- The table of contents of a book.
- The page from a dictionary.
- The page from a thesaurus.
- A puzzle.
- A maze.

We can use anything to focus our audience's attention.

And we can link it to our talk.

When we are closing the sale, the form gives us a focal point to look at and read along with the sales person.

When we are discussing bill-shock, we can have an example of a utilities bill.

Need to get people working in a team? A jigsaw puzzle can be great.

Want to grow people's vocabulary? Use the thesaurus or dictionary.

How about showing the world from a different view? Use a topographical map of the Rocky Mountains in the USA.

We can incorporate the handout into our presentation. When we use simple items from our everyday life, people feel comfortable. They can be great to trigger a key emotion or memory from our talk.

Applying a new significance to ordinary things is a clever way to have our talk last longer than just while we are speaking. And with a handout, many times they can take it home.

If we tie an emotion to the newspaper, a magazine, a bill, or a map, it will be remembered whenever they see those items again in their daily life.

What else can we use?

- A coffee cup.
- A failed invention.
- A coupon for lunch.
- A sugar packet.
- All the parts of a bicycle.
- A phone from 1995.
- A headscarf.
- A notepad.
- A bicycle tire.
- A tennis racquet.
- The parts to build a table.
- Legos.
- Matchsticks.
- Chopsticks.
- Dried spaghetti.

The list is almost never-ending. As long as we can find a way to create an emotional memory for a static object, we can use it in our talks.

And we do not need one object for everyone. We can have one item, and pass it around the room.

Or we can give small groups one item each (or one set of items to assemble).

Creativity is the key.

Match an item to a handout for the audience and the outcome for the talk.

Keep it simple, and make it memorable.

Physical Activities.

Length of time: Five to fifteen minutes.
Best time to use it: Middle.
Comfort zone scale: 5/5. Everyone likes to move, especially if they have been sitting for a while.
Humour: If people do funny things in the activity, yes.
Props: Specific to the activity.

Time to use our body.

This is the first real breach of the five-minute rule, because some physical activities like sports or games may go up to 15 minutes. If we have to relocate to a gymnasium or field, an hour or more is possible.

It can be useful to change the tone of our talk and do something physical. When any talk has gone on for more than 45 minutes, the audience is restless. It has been proven that the human mind cannot take much more information in after this amount of time. We want to keep our audience focused, paying attention or learning. So a break is necessary.

If we want to close a section of a talk or training, we can use a physical activity. It can be a great way to end the mental part of our talk. We can engage the other senses and reconnect with our bodies.

Physical exercises also get people out of their heads. They can detach from their laptop, phone or notepad. This type of activity makes them get up, breathe, soak up some fresh air and stretch their bodies. This helps them to get back into listening to our talk, more alert than before. All that mental energy focusing on listening, learning, studying or thinking can be tiring.

What can we do? Let's look at some activities. Each can take up to five minutes and provide a break for our audience. They do not need to have any other purpose. But if we do have an alternative point to make, then more preparation will be required.

Individual activities.

- Please stand up and roll your head in a circle.
- Please stand up and lean forward, then back, then side to side.
- Please stand up and pat your partner on the back.
- Please stand up, find a partner and shake their hand.
- Please stand up and give a round of applause.
- Please stand up and turn around clockwise, then counter-clockwise, then sit down.
- Please put your phone in your pocket. Turn to the person beside you and say hello.
- Please put your pen and paper down and stand up and stretch.
- Please stand up and walk to one side of the room.
- Please push your chair back and turn to the person behind you and say hello.
- Please close your laptop and stand up and look around the room.

- Please put your phone on your table and look up to the ceiling.

Group activities.

- Please pick up your chair and put it to the side of the room.

- Please leave your chair and walk to the front of the room and onto the stage one at a time.

- Please stack three chairs on top of each other.

- Please form a group of five people and sit in your chairs in a circle, facing away from each other.

- Please form a pair and get across the room without your feet touching the ground.

- Form a circle of five people and introduce yourself to the other people in your circle.

- Form a group of three people and throw the ball around your group like it is a hot potato.

- Form a group of five people and see who can do the most push-ups.

- Form a group of three people and discuss who has the most effective fitness strategy.

- Form a group of three people and discuss what the future of space travel is.

Bigger activities that need more setup and anywhere from 15 minutes to three hours.

- Play a game of musical chairs. The winner gets to speak onstage.

- Giant game of snakes and ladders.
- Rock, paper, scissors with the entire room.
- Team-building games.
- Roleplaying games.
- Scenario games.
- Compete to build a jigsaw puzzle together.
- A game of touch football.
- Mini Olympics.

Sometimes the activity is the session. In a training workshop or seminar, an entire 90-minute session might be an activity.

But in most talks, we want a five-minute physical break from the listening and writing.

We want people to enjoy the activity and have a good time.

It is important to focus on making any activity valuable. There can - and should - always be some link to the outcome of our talk. Even if we tell them that there is no link, it still has a purpose by providing a break.

Everyone gets energised when they are out of their seats.

When the audience is standing or participating in an activity, they talk to each other. In these moments, they relax and become more open. The next session of speaking becomes easier for the presenter, when the audience has had a chance to relax.

Timing for physical activities is the key. Know the exact length of time of our activity so we finish on time (or early), to get the maximum impact of our talk or training.

With a positive result from the activity, we will have a happy audience. If they are happy, they will continue listening to us. And they will be happy to do more activities.

Which we hope leads them into being happy to buy what we have to sell.

The Power of a Smile.

Length of time: Seconds.
Best time to use it: Beginning, middle and end.
Comfort zone scale: 5/5. Very easy to do.
Humour: Yes, with some variations or when reacting.
Props: None.

Cheese. :)

Our body language shows the audience how confident we are.

Our audience makes judgements about our appearance before we even open our mouth!

Our posture will be seen as confident or weak. Even the speed and style of our walking sends the audience a message.

Most speakers have no idea what their body is doing when they are on the stage. It is a unique role of course, standing and talking to a room full of people.

Controlling our body language is vital. Professional speakers practice what their body will do when they speak. They remove distractions. This makes it easier for the audience to engage with their words because their body language is congruent.

How to create positive body language.

We need to begin practicing our talks in front of a full-length mirror, to see what our body does when we speak, from head to toe.

Imagine the audience is on the other side of that mirror. There might be 10, 100, or 1,000 people. Maybe the audience is made up of our family and friends. They're counting on us to give a great talk. Everyone wants to feel like their time is well-spent.

A prospect is there to have a great presentation delivered so maybe they will buy something.

A wedding audience wants to be entertained by a funny, personal series of stories and experiences.

Everything we do with our body makes a statement.Is it positive or negative? The next step.

Your body needs to be congruent with the words coming out of your mouth.

Do we look nervous? Are our movements unsure or jerky?

Are we awkward with our eye contact? Are we getting mixed messages from the audience?

Our body language completes the message. If the body language does nothing to help the words, people will disengage. If our words match our body, the "package" is complete.

The power of a smile.

One of the simplest things we can do is smile.

When we smile, we break down barriers. We take away the initial fear that an audience can have. The personality of the speaker can be seen as dominating, arrogant, scary, wild, powerful, and knowledgeable.

- A smile brings the pressure down.
- A smile engages the crowd.

- A smile invites reciprocation.

Smiling is instinctive. People smile back when we do it first, just like looking into a mirror. And it is always up to us to lead the smiling. If we can plan to smile in our talk, we will find people in the audience that smile back. That engages them and makes everyone feel good.

When we find those people who are the first to smile, we know we have a fan in our audience. We know that we can look at them during our talk. They will reflect our emotional state back to us.

- When we smile, they will smile.
- When we are intense, they will be intensely focused.
- When we are telling a sad story, they will cry.
- And when we are enthusiastic, they will be jumping out of their chairs!

A smile can be used in a variety of moments during our talk.

- At the opening before we start to speak.
- When someone in the audience says something funny.
- When we say something positive.
- When we are nervous but want to show confidence.
- During the telling of a story that has moments of humour.
- When we make eye contact with people.
- At the end of a story.
- When we get to the end of a joke and want to keep from laughing.
- With the telling of a key point.
- When we reveal a secret.

- When someone in the crowd laughs unexpectedly.
- When there is something we are truly happy about.
- When the winner of a game or competition is announced.
- When we are finishing.
- When we thank anyone.
- When we want to be seen as a friendly person (any time).
- While giving instructions about filling in paperwork.
- When we are impatient.
- When we are frustrated.
- When we are waiting for the answer to a question from the audience.

A smile is engaging.

A smile is inviting.

A smile is never threatening or aggressive.

So does that mean our smile always looks the same?

Not at all. We need to be prepared to use different smiles, by practicing them in the mirror.

The greeting smile.

A gentle smile that shows all of our teeth. If possible, when we show our top teeth, we can pull our bottom lip lower. This will show part of our bottom teeth, and the more teeth we show, the better.

This is a very effective smile for meeting and greeting people. Think of hospitality workers, hotel reception, waiters and waitresses, and flight attendants. They all smile a big welcoming smile. This smile also looks the best in photos.

The lip smile.

Just the lips. This can be a very subtle smile. When we use this, it can be because we do not want to show a full smile. With the lip smile we show that we can use dry humour. Or react professionally while still agreeing with a joke or situation that is funny. We have to stay in control. So smiling with our lips only, even if they are just barely curling up at the edges, makes an impact.

It can also be how we smile at people who are talking. So we are seen to be listening, focused on them. It is more of a reactive or responsive smile than it is a proactive smile.

The top row smile.

When we are talking, most of the time people can see our teeth, even if they are not perfectly aligned or whiter than snow. Teeth are vital for good pronunciation of our words. Our tongue presses against them and the roof of our mouth for particular sounds.

Smiling and showing the top teeth is a general all-purpose smile, when we find something funny, or are speaking clearly and using our mouth correctly. While our audience is applauding our introduction, when we are happy in general, and when thanking the audience, this smile is appropriate.

The Cheshire Cat.

The coolest cat in the world. Everyone that has seen Alice in Wonderland knows the amazing, sometimes invisible, Cheshire Cat. An impossibly wide mouth with dozens of teeth, all shining and perfect. This smile is for those times when we are charming our audience. Also for the occasion when we want to appear "over the top" with our smile.

Often it involves a tilt of the head to the left or right, and even a flutter of the eyes. This works for men and women. People get the humour in the smile, and may laugh if it is used as part of a joke. Charm is always useful, but this smile can also help people to realise we are not taking ourselves too seriously.

All these smiles are body language tips for just one part of our body. It is worth learning more about body language.

How to Get
a Standing Ovation.

Length of time: Five minutes.
Best time to use it: Early in a talk.
Comfort zone scale: 5/5. Very easy to do.
Humour: Yes.
Props: The entire audience.

Please welcome ...

For many people, learning how to get a standing ovation is important. It may be the most valuable thing they learn in the workshop.

When they hear the speaker's introduction, they are the first person standing. This lets everyone know how much they are looking forward to the talk.

With a standing ovation, a speaker cannot help but smile. The clapping of the audience gets louder. Then, because most people are followers, the rest of the crowd stand, and clap as loud as they can. The energy is amazing.

When there are whistles, cheers, and applause, the speaker feels on top of the world.

How do we train people to give a standing ovation?

In our introduction.

If we give our Master of Ceremonies or host a script to read, 99% of the time they read it word-for-word.

Do we want our speaker to have a great opening? This is where we can make that happen. To have a standing ovation, we can simply have the host read the right words.

"So ladies and gentlemen, please stand up and give a big round of applause to welcome your next speaker, Coach Mark Davis!"

So what happens next?

The person giving the introduction is standing and clapping. Then a few people in the front row stand up, making it easy for everyone behind them to follow.

And in an audience of 10 or an audience of 1,000, this works to provide a loud and enthusiastic standing ovation.

What is the alternative?

- With a poor introduction, the audience is unsure when to clap.
- If they do not hear the name clearly, they might not even know who is coming up to speak.
- When the energy is low, there is more work for the speaker to do to build rapport.

If we walk up onstage without a strong introduction, we are off to a bad start. The talk will begin with low energy.

When you get the audience standing up, cheering and clapping, you have already won. They are excited about the speaker. They are excited about the content. Now they want the speech to go well. This is because they have just done the cheering they would do at the end of the talk. Now their expectations are high and they will be leaning forward to listen. This is the first step in building rapport.

If a standing ovation is powerful at the beginning, it is the perfect climax to a great talk at the end.

Train the host to walk up onstage after the speaker has finished. Have them say "Thank you, <speaker>!"

While the audience is applauding, the host waves their arms up and down. And loudly encourages the audience with these words. "Come on, another big round of applause to let <our speaker> know how much we appreciate <him/her>. It was great, thank you!"

A great first impression, and a great one to finish.

The Treasure Hunt.

Length of time: Five minutes setup. Fifteen minutes to three hours duration.
Best time to use it: Middle.
Comfort zone scale: 1/5. Lots of stretching and confrontation of different beliefs and fears.
Humour: No.
Props: All collected along the way. We need to write down the list for the hunt and form teams.

Get massive results quickly.

This activity is perfect for weekend events, or full-day conferences. It requires significant research and setup, and the audience will need to form teams to play.

The basic purpose of a treasure hunt is to get everyone involved. Use the energy of the activity to help them achieve what otherwise would not have been possible.

The setup for this activity.

As a presenter, we have to give the audience background information on a skill or piece of knowledge. Show how valuable it is to have it, and show the benefits of mastering it. At the same time we need to talk about the power of action, rather than listening to others.

We might talk about book knowledge vs. experience.

Or theory vs. practice.

For example:

In Singapore, a group of 70 people were in a two-day leadership boot camp. The key outcome was to get people talking to strangers and confronting a cold market of prospects.

The ultimate goal to win the treasure hunt was to collect the highest number of business cards. These would all be prospects for the people in the competition.

The prize was $500 worth of training books and CDs.

The list of items to collect included:

- As many business cards or name cards as they could collect.
- Special deals and offers for the entire group.
- Free samples from food stores.
- One new sale of their product.
- Proof they had made 10 prospecting phone calls.
- A free gift like a pen, book, or sticker for everyone in their team.

The winner was the person who collected the most business cards. He collected 168 cards in 3 hours. It was impressive. And because he collected so many more than everyone else, they wanted to know how he did it. He shared with the group how he did it.

Our winner loved to compete, and loved to win. He chose the task of starting short conversations with people and exchanging cards, without committing to a long conversation. He was honest, saying that he was in a competition. And he was energetic and positive, making eye contact and offering his own card first. He thanked the person for their card, and kept moving. He was on fire.

One of the principles at work here was explained to everyone. People are naturally reciprocal. If we offer something, they want to give something back. A business card is one of the simplest forms of exchange. And in Singapore, everyone carries their card with them.

Every person that participated in the treasure hunt created more prospects for their business by participating. The winner just showed why he was already successful and going to be even more successful.

What sort of treasure hunts can we create?

- Tourist information in a new city.
- Free samples, coupons and deals.
- Picking up financial information from banks and investment companies.
- Getting data and minutes offers for mobile phones.
- Finding the price of certain items in department stores.
- Getting an item for under $1 from a department store toy section.
- Collecting business cards.
- Things from the "wild" like sticks, leaves, fruits, flowers.

The key is to relate the hunt to a purpose in the talk.

Debrief the treasure hunt so everyone gets the value from it.

Have a prize worth winning so people feel compelled to participate at 100%.

Visuals and Props.

Length of time: Two minutes.
Best time to use: Early in a talk.
Comfort zone scale: 1/5. If the props are unusual or new, people do not like to engage with them unless they know they cannot break them or use them incorrectly.
Humour: Not necessarily.
Props: The visual item.

Use the power of a picture.

Using pictures and other visuals is a great way to entertain the audience.

When they are bored with looking at us, we can focus their attention on a screen, slide, flipchart, whiteboard or other visual object.

TED talks capture our imagination immediately because they have a spotlight on the speaker. They also often have key visuals on the screen or on the stage.

In one talk, an amazing visual was the tracking of flight data to show flight patterns appearing like a fountain of fireworks across North America. The data showed planes taking off and landing. There were flight path holding patterns, the morning and evening rush hours. And then the screen went dark with all the planes going to sleep around midnight. They were amazing images, and it was totally fascinating to watch over 30,000 flights in one visual representation.

Integrating a visual item into our talk is definitely a positive strategic move.

The visual or picture or movie can be worth more than 1,000 words.

Some speakers use the visual element to insert humour into their talk. Maybe they use facial gestures and movement, or a key prop.

Some visuals:

- A photo inserted into the PowerPoint presentation.
- A series of images on the screen that tell the point of our story.
- A picture that tells a thousand words, and can also reinvigorate a dying presentation.

Need examples of what to show?

If our presentation is about financial independence, and owning a big home:

- Put up a picture of a mansion in Beverly Hills.
- Or a yacht off a Caribbean island.
- Or a resort at Aspen in the snow.

If we are talking about being a successful speaker, showing a room full of people with one person speaking shows what a big audience looks like.

Sometimes we need to give the audience a visual to help our words make sense.

When a concept is brand-new, having a visual can make it real and assist with goal-setting, dream-building and planning the future.

When we talk about mastering a skill - showing a photo of others using that skill can be key.

When we share our own experiences, people do not like to see us in the photographs. Ever remember visiting a friend who had just returned from a vacation? They are sure that we will be interested in watching thousands of photos of where they went, but we aren't. How do we feel? We might be bored, or even resentful.

It is better to put up photos with other people in them, or of the location or experience alone. Then the audience can place themselves into the picture, and are more inspired to want to visit.

When we put up images, we want them to be the best quality possible. High-resolution photos and high-definition videos give the experience of being immersed in the image. Blurry or small images look cheap and unprofessional.

What are some other visuals we can use to grab the audience's attention?

- Balloons. Blow them up, have them available in different shapes, or pop them; balloons are a versatile visual prop.

- Streamers. If we are celebrating something, the short-term effect of making a mess with streamers and ribbons and even confetti can create a lasting memory. People will look back at that moment in time positively and remember what we said.

- A giant beach ball. At sports events, balls are thrown around stadiums because even though the crowd loves their sport, sometimes it can get boring. The beach ball has everyone feeling like a child again, with enthusiasm, joy, and a touch of rebellion.

- Any sports equipment - dumbbells, bow and arrow, tennis racquet. Sports are great metaphors for what we do in life: building our strength and resilience, shooting for our goals, or firing down an ace in our presentations.

- Using volunteers on the stage. Volunteers provide entertainment to the audience. They come onstage for the attention and the extra value of being the subject of the speech for a few minutes. They also have a different personality, voice, clothing and attitude than the speaker. All of this provides an interesting contrast to what we are saying. So that engages the audience, as they want to see what will happen.

- Videos engage more senses. Videos need to be short clips, or incredibly interesting. If they are too long or boring, they become the problem rather than the solution. And if the video is worse than the speaker? Then there is a massive challenge to keep the audience paying attention.

What if our talk is quite short and there is no ideal visual element to show?

- Maybe we do not have a PowerPoint or access to the internet.

- Maybe we do not have an array of sporting equipment to use.

- And maybe we do not have the right environment to ask for a volunteer.

Then, writing is an alternative.
What we write becomes the focal visual element.

Most training rooms will have a whiteboard or flipchart.

Using the visual medium to write down key words and phrases gives us a chance to have a new visual point of focus.

If there is nothing for us to write on?

Then we can ask people in our audience to write things down. The writing gives them something to look at with purpose.

No paper?

We can ask them to write a note on their phone. Or research something on the internet. Or ask "Siri" about a key fact.

There is always a way to incorporate a visual element, as long as we are creative and have planned for all potential outcomes.

Here are a few more items we can use to get the audience engaged visually:

- Book
- Pen
- Hat
- Shoe
- T-shirt
- Tie
- Jewelry
- Yoga mat
- Hair tie/ribbon
- Pack of cards
- Sunglasses
- Brick
- Window frame

- Phone
- Tablet
- Laptop
- Watch
- Clock
- Chair
- Table
- Microphone
- Photo frame
- Polaroid camera
- Coffee cup
- Water bottle
- Clipboard
- Notepad
- Handbag
- Satchel
- Backpack
- A creaky stage
- Steps
- Lighting including spotlights
- Ball
- Plane
- Box of matches
- USB
- CD
- LP Record
- Cassette
- Hotel stuff

- Abacus
- Monopoly board or other board game
- Photos

The sky is the limit, and every visual can be an item that creates a permanent memory of our talk, our key point, and us.

Multimedia.

Length of time: Five minutes.
Best time to use it: Middle.
Comfort zone scale: 1/5-5/5. Very easy to do. But difficult to do well. It helps to be an actor or natural performer.
Humour: Yes.
Props: Some technology - phone, projector, laptop, iPad or similar.

We can use technology in our presentation to entertain our audience.

Videos, photos, music and interactive communication are all good options.

We do it all the time when we are alone.

It is possible to watch a live event from any smartphone or computer. We can log in and watch the live stream on Periscope, Facebook, Meerkat, Ustream, or YouTube. Many trainings, webinars and conference calls are done this way now.

We can broadcast our presentation this way.

What if we did this in our event? Make a phone call to a friend and have that conversation broadcast live for the whole room to hear? Now that would be interesting. It would be like a giant speaker phone.

Video.

There are many ways we can use video in our presentation. But the key is to use it sparingly. We do not want the novelty effect taking over our talk. People will also revert to their natural TV-watching posture and attitude if it is too long. They will get bored and want to change the channel.

The best video is interactive. A powerful way to entertain with video is to call someone. On Skype, we can make a video call and connect with someone across the room or around the world.

With streaming video, we can broadcast our presentation and include the audience. They can participate in what is being shared and create the content in real time.

We can also have them do their own video, and either create it on the spot, or broadcast a prepared presentation.

Live video is great, and live video with a script is even better to build confidence with using video as a tool.

Here are some topics for a great video section in our talk or presentation:

- 30-second sale item.
- Sales pitch.
- Product endorsements.
- Interview with another student or the presenter.
- Exercise demonstration like Yoga or Pilates.
- Demonstration of how a product works.
- Telling a short joke.
- Making an invitation.
- Proposing a date.
- Offering a deal.

- Demonstrating something on a computer.
- A quick recipe.
- Roleplay.

Do not get stuck trying to get it right.

Most people never finish making a video because they feel it has to be perfect.

This is a mistake. An amateur video is the way of the world today. We all watch them on Facebook and YouTube. We see people streaming video live and even doing conferences on Skype.

Every video we do gets better. With practice and feedback, we can improve.

Apps and Software.

Length of time: Five minutes to download, install and use.
Best time to use it: Early and middle.
Comfort zone scale: 1/5-5/5. Most people with a smartphone will have downloaded an app before. For those who have not, working with a partner can help them.
Humour: No.
Props: Phone or tablet or laptop, internet, screen.

Download.

Here is a great activity to get people involved with their technology in a practical way.

Every day millions of apps are installed onto smartphones and tablets from either the App Store or Google Play.

People download software to their computer to run new programs and manage their business more effectively. (Or they have their IT department or children do it.)

Knowing all this, we can do what the audience likes to do, and achieve a practical goal at the same time.

When we teach a principle or share a great idea, it is helpful for us to follow up with action. This will create a physical memory to match the concept or idea being talked about.

The action can be downloading an app or installing software. Or we can give a list of apps and programs to download. They can be for everyday actions done on a phone like editing photos, chatting, or booking flights and hotels.

For example:

What if we talked about ridesharing? Many people in the audience will raise their hand when we ask if they have heard of rideshare companies like Uber, GoCatch and Lyft. Fewer people will raise their hand if they are asked if they have the app on their phone or have used the services.

To add value to our talk, we can assist them in downloading the app, creating an account, and receiving a referral bonus or introductory offer.

We might talk about travel, and how some people rent out their spare room or their entire house when they go on holiday. Some people have heard of companies like AirBnB and HomeAway and Couchsurfing. But not everyone has used them.

We encourage them to register for an account with our referral code. This gets them a bonus and also gives us a referral commission.

Could this be a way to make extra cash when we speak?

Think of other apps and software that people could download.

For communication:

- WhatsApp
- Skype
- Telegram
- Viber

- Cyber Dust

How about these for photos and videos:

- Fotor
- Adobe Photoshop
- Instagram
- Capture

And these for writing:

- Paper
- Notability
- Pages
- Numbers
- Keynote
- Microsoft Word
- Google Sheets

What about video and social media?

- Youtube
- Periscope
- Meerkat
- TED
- Vine
- Ustream
- Snapchat

Not every app or program has a bonus structure for encouraging people to get an account.

But if our purpose is to offer something of value to people, we just might get a "thank you." Apps and useful programs and websites can save people money, make people money or even change their lives.

What else could we suggest they do on their phone or laptop?

- Subscribe at our website.
- Join a Facebook group.
- Like a page.
- Watch a quick video.
- Rate and review a book.
- Register a domain name.
- Open an advertising account with Google.
- Create a fan page.

Use technology in our talk and people will not feel guilty about looking at their phone or tablet. They will have received a free idea or concept that could be useful to them in the future.

Photos.

Length of time: Two to fifteen minutes.
Best time to use it: Throughout the presentation.
Comfort zone scale: 5/5. Everyone takes photos.
Humour: Depends on the setup of the photo.
Props: Camera/smartphone.

Snap!

Today more than ever the phone has the camera for everyday life and events.

In our audience, we can be confident that nearly 80% of the room will have a phone. Most will take good photos. And these photos can be messaged, emailed, posted online and viewed around the world within seconds.

Knowing this, we can create simple activities using the technology sitting in their hands or pockets.

It is important to remember that the audience members like to do things they are comfortable with. Give them permission to take photos in our talk and we can unleash a flood of free promotion. Be sure to get tagged in the photos.

Promoting our event, our talk, our seminar or workshop can be hard. But when the audience is taking photos and referencing us and recommending us, it is the best possible endorsement.

What is the best way to use the camera?

Suggest the audience takes photos of themselves. Selfies are the best ego boost and the best proof of attendance and participation. Suggest they take a photo with us.

Give them a #hashtag or our social media username to ensure we get as much exposure as possible.

Remind them how to spell our name so we show up in search results in the future.

Encourage them to take multiple photos so they can post the best ones.

What can we ask them to photograph?

- Take a photo of the crowd when the talk is in session.
- Take a photo at the break of the venue lobby.
- Take a photo of themselves at the photo booth.
- Take a photo of the speaker and with the speaker.
- Take a photo with their friends.
- Take a photo of the amazing patterns in the carpet on the floor.
- Take a photo of the ornate ceiling.
- Take a photo of the drapes on the walls.
- Take a photo of the artwork in the foyer.
- Take a photo of the hardworking students doing an activity.
- Take a photo of the team they formed in the activity they won.
- Take a photo of the leader of the team.

- Take a photo of the winners of any games or activities.
- Take a photo of the standing ovation at the end of the day.
- Take a photo with the organiser.
- Take a photo with your team and the speaker.
- Take a photo up on the stage with the audience behind you.
- Take a photo of the empty room after everyone has left.

Once they take photos, remember to tell them they can post them anywhere. There is no such thing as bad advertising, and the candid photos they take without us posing make us look more natural.

This is all good publicity for our talk, lecture, training or wedding speech.

And if we want to speak for a living, this provides more material online for people when they are searching for us.

Objections.

Length of time: Five minutes.
Best time to use it: In the middle or towards the end.
Comfort zone scale: 1/5-3/5. Some confrontation in the activity.
Humour: No.
Props: None.

Objection!

When we close, we want to have the biggest issues already out of the way.

If we have an expensive product, we need to talk about value.

If we have something never seen before, we can talk about early adopters and pioneers.

And if we have a product that is just like everyone else's, we can talk about our price and terms to make it easy to buy.

Objections can strike fear in a salesperson's heart. Some look forward to having a battle they must win. This turns audiences into adversaries. Dealing with objections before they arise takes this problem away and helps us to have a professional presentation.

If we don't prepare, our sales process turns into outright war.

What if we're not selling? There are probably questions about our presentation, any time we are leading to a decision or action for the audience.

If we deliver a talk that will stimulate questions and/or objections, it makes sense to be prepared.

For fewer questions and limited objections, we need a strategy. This is to confront those questions and objections during the body of our talk.

How do we handle objections while we present?

- "So last week someone asked me … And here is what I shared with them."
- "The #1 question I get when I talk about this web portal is … and here is what I say."
- "When we look at this issue, there are obvious challenges like…"
- "Some people look at this product and think about the price."
- "It has been said that there is just not enough time in our lives to attend another conference."

Our presentation should have already answered every possible objection. When this happens, we don't need to worry about any surprises at the end of our talk.

We can build in the typical challenges that customers expect. We can show how we have solved problems for other clients. This will show that everything that comes along is something we can handle.

Every question the audience could ask - we should answer before they need to ask it.

Every objection needs to be managed before they can provide any emotional ammunition. We do not need any bombs dropped during our close.

Because if we don't cover the objectionable parts of our presentation early, they'll bring it up at the end, or in a question after we close.

It is better to cover the questions and objections early. Then we can move confidently towards our close. It can be awkward when someone raises their hand at the precise time where we most want to get a decision.

Will people still bring up questions and objections? It's possible. But if we prepared properly, the issue was already addressed earlier in our talk. We can refer back to it. There is not the same emotional energy that a surprise question or objection creates.

The end.

In this book I covered many different ways to entertain and engage our audience. Will you want to use every technique? Of course not.

You will want to choose techniques that work for your style. Or, pick the techniques that fit the audience and the speech you will make.

- A great opening gives us a chance with our audience.

- A great close only works if our audience is still alive.

- It is the middle of our talk where we deliver our value.

Unfortunately, our audience has to be kept alive with entertainment and engagement. A dead audience will never hear the value we wish to deliver.

So I wish you good fortune in your speaking engagements. I hope you can use many of these entertainment and engagement techniques in your future speeches.

- Mark

P.S. Thank you for purchasing and reading my book. I hope you received many solutions to the audience engagement challenges we all face. Before you go, I would like to ask a favour. Would you take just one minute and leave a sentence or two reviewing this book online? Your review can help others choose what they read next. Your review would be greatly appreciated.

What next?

There are a few free resources you can take advantage of.

Be sure to subscribe to the Public Speaking tips at www.markdavis.com.au

Take advantage of the other books in the Public Speaking Series at www.amazon.com/author/markdavisaustralia

Join the Public Speaking Mastermind group in Facebook. www.facebook.com/groups/publicspeakingmastermind

Mark is available for speaking at conferences and conventions, as well as private coaching. For anything else, please email **mark@markdavis.com.au** for details.

Made in the USA
Columbia, SC
14 September 2021

45451363R00089